Anonymous

Home Memories And Other Poems

Anonymous

Home Memories And Other Poems

ISBN/EAN: 9783744717694

Printed in Europe, USA, Canada, Australia, Japan

Cover: Foto ©Thomas Meinert / pixelio.de

More available books at **www.hansebooks.com**

HOME MEMORIES

AND OTHER POEMS.

BY

L B. L.

TO

THE RIGHT HONOURABLE

THE LADY MARY TOPHAM,

THE NOBLEST, TRUEST, AND DEAREST

OF HER FRIENDS,

THIS LITTLE VOLUME

(FULL OF RECORDS OF THE PAST)

IS INSCRIBED,

WITH GRATEFUL AFFECTION,

BY

L. B. L.

May, 1873.

A FEW WORDS OF PREFACE.

WHILST I am yet amongst the living, I believe these Fragmentary Poems will not be devoid of interest to the kind eyes which will peruse them ; and when my place on earth "*shall know me no more,*" all I would *ask* is this :--

> "Speak gently of the Dead ; for, judge who will,
> The Loving Heart which beat so high is still."

In the better words of the Italian Poet—

> " Fermossi al fin quel cor
> Chè balzò tanto ! "

CONTENTS.

—

SONGS OF LOCH GOIL.

	PAGE
Ben Donich	3
Lake Lochan	4
Duncan	4
Glen Glasslet, or Drimsynie Cave	5
The Highland Storm	7
My Highland Home	9
The Sportsman's Song—The Hunt of the Roe. . . .	9
A Sportsman's Song—The Ptarmigan	10
Lonely Thoughts	11
The Return	12
The Two Leaves	13
The Wild Gheen Tree	14
The Sapphire Lake	15
A Boating Song	16
Sea-shore Musings	17
Dear Old Ben Donich	17
Loch Goil by Moonlight	19
Adieu, Loch Goil	20
Gem of the Highlands	21

FLOWERS OF AUCHENGRAY.

Introductory Lines	25
Scotch Thistle	25

	PAGE
The White Heather	25
The Heather	26
The Lady's Mantle	27
Lines	27
The Ragged Robin, or Wild Clarkia	27
The Lady Rush	28
The White Harebell	29
The Silver Leaf	29
The Grass of Parnassus	30
White Cud-weed	30
On some Sea-weeds	31
The St. John's Wort	31
The Wood-Sage	32
On some Wild Flowers gathered by Sir A. and Lady G.	32
Balm-wood Fig-wort	32
Golden Rod ; or, Summer Farewell	33
Frozen Fern Leaves	33
Wild Bouquet (gathered by the Lady M. T.)	34
Epilobium, or Willow Herb	34
The Foxglove's Bridal	35
On Another Visit	36
Wild Bouquet	37
The Sea Pink, or Thrift	37
Snowdrop, or Galanthus	38
Ferns covered with Ice and Hoar Frost	39
To Heathcote	40
The Forget-me-not Bed at Auchengray	41
Minnie's Wild Bouquet	41
In Ricordanza	42
Flowers by the Lake	43
June Thoughts	44

CONTENTS.

	PAGE
To James B—, Esq.	45
The Alpine Walk	46
The Last Flowers gathered in my Scottish Home	48

MISCELLANEOUS POEMS.

Fairlight Glen	51
Lines suggested by the Massacre at Hango Head, etc.	55
The Stranger's Adieu to Moray Land	57
Moray Land	59
The Shepherd's Chief Mourner	60
Solitary Musings	62
The Butterfly at Sea	63
The Nightingale in the Acacia Tree	66
The Little Miners	67
Forest Song	67
Summer Days	68
God's Sunshine	69
To the Robins	70
Youthful Memories	70
Warning	73
Pleading	76
Thoughts on the Lamented Death of the Right Hon. Lord George Bentinck	77
Hagar	79
Songs	80
A May Song	81
A Song	82
A Life	83
Meditations in Illness	84
Spring Fancies	86
Lines written July, 1871	87

	PAGE
Two Christmas Songs .	88
Christmas Song	89
Farewell to the Old Year .	90
On the death of little Tiny .	91
The Weary Heart	92
Marino Faliero	94
Lines written in the first page of the " Book of Beauty " in 1841	98
They cannot return . .	100
Hymn—Adoration .	101
Faith	101
Sympathy	102
Heaven .	103
Supplication	103
Words written for Jacques Blumenthal's beautiful melody " Les Deux Anges "	104
Voices	105
Forbearance	106
Cheer up, sad Heart .	107
Mercy	108
A Hymn	109
Written in a Suffering Hour .	109
Simple Words of Comfort . .	110
Alone	111
Sabbath Bells	113
Lines	113
Self-questionings	114
Desolation	115
May Thoughts at Chetnole	116

SONGS OF LOCH GOIL.

BEN DONICH.

BEN DONICH! Ben Donich!* thou mountain so
grand!
Thou art one of the giants of Scotia's fair land !
Thou hast loftier brothers, defying the storm,
But *to me,* none so fondly familiar in form :
Their glens may be deeper, their heather more
bright,
But never so lovely or dear to my sight.
So happy I've been at thy foot, I could dwell
Thus for years 'neath thy shadow : then kindly fare-
well !

      *   *   *   *

Ben Donich! I've gazed on thee; Morning and
Eve
I've seen thee thy first snowy garland receive ;
Where the grouse and the ptarmigan love to abide.
And the roe-deer bound free o'er thy steep rocky
side—
Looking down on Loch Goil's sapphire waters—that
lake
Whose name doth the soul of sweet Poesy wake—
So happy I've been at thy foot—I could dwell
Thus for years 'neath thy shadow—then fondly fare-
well !

     * Ben Donich, the highest mountain near Loch Goil.

LAKE LOCHAN.

THERE are spots in our Highlands so lovely !
  Enchantment rules over the scene—
That Lake, 'mongst the mountains all lonely,
  No lips can describe it ! I ween ;
    So bright and still, half-way up to the skies,
    That lake in its silvery radiance lies,
And gently rebukes old Ben Lochan's frown
Which scowls on Ben Viula's rival crown ;
O Lochan ! sweet Lochan ! thou'rt haunting me yet ;
Should I ne'er more behold thee, I could not forget !

Though the way to approach thee be weary,
  O'er precipice, river, and fen,
The waterfall's music is cheery,
  Dashing down from thy wild native glen.
    Like some fair girl guarded by warriors stern,
    To thy smile, from the cold dark rocks we turn
And think, though the tempest may round thee roar,
There must ever be peace on thy tranquil shore—
O Lochan ! sweet Lochan ! thou'rt haunting me yet ;
Should I ne'er more behold thee, I could not forget.

DUNCAN.

(*Our old Gamekeeper.*)

I'VE a Friend in the Highlands, of humble degree,
Far more to my taste than a courtier would be,
There's a dignity sits on his weather-stain'd brow,
And worth all the mock homage of fashion's cold bow
Is his kindly " *Good Morrow.*" Respect in his mien—
As he stands, cap in hand, with his smile so serene ;

Or follows his master with dogs and with gun ;
Oh ! of Nature's own gentlemen, Duncan is one.

I've a Friend in the Highlands, though poor in degree,
He might teach a bright lesson to you and to me
Of cheerful contentment, of love most sincere—
A mind that seeks Heaven, and faith to revere !
From his grand native mountains a spirit he's caught,
A gaze that *looks upward*, with hopefulness fraught.
He works hard from the dawn to the setting of sun,
But of Nature's own gentlemen, Duncan is one !

I've a Friend in the Highlands, of lowly degree,
And his honest old face aye is welcome to me !
Oft a bunch of wild heather and sweet gale in hand
He'll present with the air of a prince of the land !
Up the steep rocky mountains he fearlessly springs,
The eagle and hawk from their eyry he brings ;
How gladsome his eye when such trophies he's won :
Oh ! of Nature's own gentlemen, Duncan is one !

Aug., 1854.

———◆———

GLEN GLASSLET, OR DRIMSYNIE CAVE.

GLEN GLASSLET ! in thy woodland bowers
I've pass'd a thousand pleasant hours ;
And who methinks could look on thee
Nor revel in thy scenery ?
A combination, sweet and grand,
Which makes thee seem like Fairy Land,
Of mountain, streamlet, dell and rock,
The broad expanse of yon fair loch,
The beetling cliff above the burn,
Whose banks laugh out at Spring's return

With many a varied floral gem,
Wood-sorrel on its coral stem,
The primrose pale, and celandine,
And hyacinth with scent divine ;
Forget-me-not with soft tears wet,
And columbine, and violet,
Succeeded, as the year grows old,
By Summer wealth of bloom untold !

         *   *   *   *

Oh ! when the heat grows faint—how rare
To Glasslet's grotto to repair !
Where no disturbing sound shall come,
Save the gay insect's busy hum,
Or startled tread of doe and fawn
Within the leafy covert borne—
How sweet, 'midst music of the streams,
To give the rein to fancy's dreams !
All haunting griefs and cares forgot
In this romantic sylvan spot,
While visions, not of this dull world,
Are to our mental gaze unfurl'd ;
Ah mortal ! chide them not away,
For brief those fairy visions' sway !

         *   *   *   *

     The torrent comes rushing
         O'er rocky bed,
     The wild roses blushing
         Above my head.
They hang in festoons from the wood-nymph's grot—
Full surely the dryads must own this spot!
       Hark ! I hear them now
       In each whispering bough,

And their frolic laugh rises above the wave!
  Sweet the elfin sound,
  As it swells around,
And fills with wild music the mossy cave.
   Listen! hush! listen!
   It echoes the woods among,
  The leaves in the sunshine glisten
   As they bend to the wood-nymph's song,
 *   *   *   *

  In the mountain burn,
   In the forest gloom,
  In the feathery fern,
   'Neath its fan-like plume,
Where the foxglove rings his gay chime of bells,
Yon brawling stream lulling, the wood-nymph dwells;
Never will she her deep spells reveal,
Never shall mortal her rich lore steal;
But all ye who worship rock, wood, and wave,
Your homage pay to Drimsynie's Cave.

        1853.

THE HIGHLAND STORM.

(HELL'S GLEN.)

A STORM is on the mountain brow—'tis coming on
  apace;
Haste! haste! and let us strive to gain some safe and
  sheltered place;
A thousand streams are rushing down the dark hill's
  seamèd side;
The storm fiends on the hurricane in ruthless fury
  ride.

Look up, look up ! can'st thou discern no little speck
    of blue ?
No ! nought save murky darkness meets the dim be-
    wildered view ;
The thunder loudly peals above, with lightning flash
    between—
Our Highland glen has never shown a sterner, wilder
    scene.

Oh, luckless wanderer, trust amid the perils of the
    hour
In Him whose might alone can shield and stem the
    tempest's power ;
What, though the eagle's scream doth bode a death-
    cry in the gale,
Proceed undaunted on 'thy way—why should thy
    spirit fail ?

He thinks, while struggling manfully against the pelt-
    ing storm,
Of his own hearth-fire's cheerful blaze—of some be-
    loved form,
Some faithful heart that's watching for his well-
    known step to come,—
O God ! protect the wanderer, and guide him safely
    home !

But now the air hath clearer grown ; light pierces
    through the shroud,
And Hope's bright rainbow arch begins—the " Bow
    · set in the Cloud ;"
Like baffled hosts, dark vapours fast are driven
    athwart the sky ;
Our " Highland Glen " doth smile again ; the tempest
    hath passed by.

MY HIGHLAND HOME.

THE mountains!—glorious mountains!
  How beautiful are ye!
The mountains! oh, the mountains!
  Familiar friends to me!

How I love my Highland home!
Where the waterfalls rush madly down,
And the snow-wreath, with a brilliant crown,
  Adorns each rocky dome.
There the eagle wings his towering flight,
  Soaring through the deep blue sky;
And the lake below sleeps calm and bright,
  Or tosses wild and high.

I know all the hills by name,
And their frowning heights so sternly grand,
What can vie with thee!—romantic land?
  In thy beauty, aye, the same!
Thy forests deep, where the dark pines wave
  Oer the red deer's couch of fern,
And thy thousand crystal streams which lave
  Banks of flowers at Spring's return.

———◆———

THE SPORTSMAN'S SONG.

THE HUNT OF THE ROE.

HARK! to the merry horn,
  As it sounds " *To the woods away!* "
It calls the loiterers on,
  For the deer must be slain this day!

The lovely creatures pant on,
  Nor slack their lightning pace ;
In vain ! for the *unerring Manton*
  Soon ends the exciting chase.

While the sportsman's cry is " FOLLOW,
  Follow ! follow me !
By stream, through glen and hollow,
  The stately roe-deer flee !

O'er the mountain torrent bounding,
  In fancied safety lain,
You shall hear my bugle sounding,
  " THE WILD ROE-DEER IS SLAIN !"
Then follow ! follow ! onward !
  Brave comrades side by side ;
On our stalwart shoulders " Homeward,"
  We'll bear our spoils in pride.
By waterfall and fountain,
  Still follow ! follow still !
O'er moorland, and o'er mountain,
  By river, and by rill !
We'll track the stately quarry,
  And step by step we'll go,
And until nightfall tarry,
  BUT WE'LL CARRY HOME THE ROE !

———◆———

A SPORTSMAN'S SONG.

THE PTARMIGAN.

BEN DONICH wears his cap of snow—
  A crown of dazzling splendour—
While the foaming torrents flung below,
  Their subject homage render !

" *Hurrah*, we'll have glorious sport to-day ;
   Let him climb the hill who can !
On ! over those sparkling heights away,
   For the white-plumed Ptarmigan !"

The pretty birds ! how still they lie !
   On their couch of silvery whiteness ;
Nor dream that a foot can climb so high,
   Or an eye pierce through the brightness.
Hurrah ! o'er the dark ravines we'll cross,
   Where the clear stream lately ran,
O'er the slippery rocks, o'er the frozen moss,
   For the milk-white ptarmigan.

'Tis a bird that's fit for a *Monarch's* feast,
   If true the old tradition,
That *he who doth* THE FIRST TIME taste
   Shall win his heart's ambition ! *
And the sportsman's wish, 'tis " th' unerring aim,"
   With " SUCCESS " for his talisman,
Then " *Hurrah !* " in pursuit of our mountain game,
   Of the snow-white " Ptarmigan."

———•———

LONELY THOUGHTS.

   THOU art not near me,
   Thou canst not hear me ;—
Yet I say, " *Bless thee ! my own love, good night !*"
   Fondly I'm yearning
   For thy returning ;
Thou art my sunbeam, my joy, and delight !

* In the Highlands the Ptarmigan is called the " Wishing Bird."

Little reck I of the wind or the weather
So that we spend all the seasons together.
The Summer's fierce heat or the Winter's bleak chill,
If but my own loved one be with me still.
    Yes, though thou'rt absent,
      Still in my heart,
    Thou'rt ever present,
      And bearest thy part.
In every thought, whether mournful or bright,
" So I sigh softly, *Heaven bless thee ; good-night !*"
    *   *   *   *

    I open my casement
    When morning is come,
The sun shines on mine, and on many a home ;
    But the light in my bosom
      Is all clouded o'er,
    Till thou, my "own loved one,"
      Art with me once more!
    O'er mountain, glen, vale,
    Night spreads her dark veil ;
Stars twinkle o'er the lake calmly and bright ;
    Thou art not near me,
    Thou canst not hear me ;
Softly sigh, " *Bless thee ! my own love ! Good-night !*"
                     Drimsynie, 1854.

THE RETURN.

HE'S "coming home again !" in a very little while
I shall see those blue eyes glisten, I shall see that
    sunny smile ;
In the joy of his return, I forget our parting pain,
And my heart is full of bliss, for "he's
                Coming home again."

His favourite steed which droop'd, when his master
    was away,
Will lift his head once more in pride, and give a joyous
    neigh
When the hand, whose fond caress it knows, is laid
    upon its mane—
Oh! every creature loves him, and he's
                    Coming home again.

The echo of his gun, shall amidst the hills resound,
And the sportsman's cheery music, call to huntsman
    and to hound ;
While many a kindly " welcoming" returns his
    greeting free—
Each kind word shall be precious—*for he's*
                    All the world to me.

There *may* be colder natures, which would scorn the
    anxious fear
That follows still the absent one—so exquisitely dear!
Who'd think 'twas idle folly thus *to care* till love
    grows pain—
THEY cannot feel the ecstacy of
                    " *Coming home again.*"

THE TWO LEAVES.

THAT " *Life is like a River,*"
    Thou'st often said to me—
Still floating on for ever
    Towards Time's boundless sea !

And *we*—the leaves borne swiftly on
  Adown its course which glide—
So let it be, belovèd one,
  Thus ever, side by side!

        *   *   *

By Summer airs blown lightly,
  Their voyage began in play—
And flowery banks smiled brightly
  On their enamell'd way.
But ah! the storms too quickly come
  And roughly onward glide—
Yet *float together, faithful home;*   ·
  Still ever—side by side!

————

THE WILD GHEEN TREE.

COME! where the bluebell's growing,
  'Neath the Gheen tree's silver bloom,
And watch the clear lake flowing,
  Whilst we breathe its sweet perfume:
Oh! ye loved—and far away—
  Would ye were here with me!
Passing the hours of the Summer day
  Under the wild Gheen tree.

        *   *   *   *

Beneath thy snowy blossoms,
  Where revels the forest bee,
Thoughts steal into our bosoms
  Mingled with grief and glee.
Spirit! whose whispers take
  Love's message to the heart!
For true affection's sake,
  Link them—the "*far apart.*"

        *   *   *   *

Oh! tell them—when the soft west wind
    Comes rustling through the leaves—
Of one—whose tender memories bind
    By that voice which ne'er deceives.
Oh! ye loved, and "*far away*,"
    Would ye were here with me.
Passing the hours of the Summer day
    Under my wild Gheen tree!

THE SAPPHIRE LAKE.

(LOCH GOIL)

YON sapphire Lake, serenely bright!
    When is it loveliest?
When it sleeps so soft in the calm moonlight,
    Each wave with a diamond crest?
Or in the early morning hours,
    When its dazzling waters foam,
Kissing the sea-Pink's rosy flowers,
    Close to the Mermaid's home.
Where the fisher seeks his finny prey,
    Singing his song the while,
And all nature basks in the Summer ray;
    Even the grand-old mountains smile?
Or when the Autumnal gale doth sweep
    Down thy rock-bound shore in might,
Lashing to fury thy bosom deep,
    And making thee black as night.
In every season, in every mood,
    Thou still enchantest me!
Nor can I deem it *solitude*,
    When thus I look on thee.

Sweet sapphire Lake! ever loveliest
  Of all silver Lakes that shine—
But when gazed on *with eyes we love the
    best,*
  Oh then! THOU DOST SEEM DIVINE!

————◆————

A BOATING SONG.

NOW Boatmen, row us gallantly!
  Gallantly, gaily on!
The air doth blow so pleasantly,
  Now the sultry noon is gone.
Row—row us o'er the sparkling wave,
  How sweet o'er the lake to glide;
Deep, deep beneath the mermaid's cave,
  Her treasures unseen doth hide.
Chaplets of pearl, as white as snow,
  She doth conceal beneath;
And many a precious gem below,
  To·bind old Ocean's wreath.

  *   *   *   *

Swift o'er the lake so dark and deep,
  Our pleasure-bark impel;
The mountain shadows calmly sleep
  On her heaving bosom's swell.
So Boatmen! row us gallantly,
  Gallantly, gaily on!
And while the air blows pleasantly,
  We'll sing our evening song.

SEA-SHORE MUSINGS.

AWAY, away, to the wild sea-shore !
  There we'll seek in some sparry cave
Bright shells ; our rich treasure from Ocean-store,
  The legacy of the wave !
I sigh for the breath of the Ocean air ;
  For the sight of the Ocean flowers !
And as graceful wreaths in *her* realms there are,
  As we boast in our inland bowers.
Oh ! I *love* the sea when my thoughts are *sad ;*
  They're sooth'd by its measured swell ;
And the sparkling foam, when my heart is glad,
  Of congenial joy doth tell.

    *   *   *   *

Ah ! when *one* dear hand lies clasp'd in mine,
  As along the shore we stray ;
How my spirit laughs at the foaming brine,
  And exults with the sparkling spray.
And when wandering thither, sometimes alone,
  Musing pensive o'er words *most dear,*
There is sympathy in the billow's moan,
  As its murmurs meet mine ear.
Yes, I love the sea ! when my thoughts are sad,
  They are *sooth'd* by its measured swell,
And its sparkling foam, when my heart is glad,
  Of a kindred joy doth tell.

DEAR OLD BEN DONICH.

DEAR old Ben Donich, who can tell
  The secrets thou dost keep ?
The wild thyme and the pimpernel,
  Where browse the Highland sheep,

Were press'd by different feet of yore —
    Poor hunted fugitives !
Who, when Prince Charlie's cause was o'er,
    Fled hither for their lives.

Less hard of heart than ruthless man,
    Thy mountain bosom gave
Safe shelter to the wounded then,
    In many a friendly cave.
A heather couch for each spent form,
    Drink from thy fountains clear,
While far away might rage the storm
    Unheeded by the ear.

Dear old Ben Donich ! o'er thy crest
    The eagle spreads his wings—
The ptarmigan doth build her nest,
    And roe-deer seek thy springs.
Like some bold loving brother, thou
    Near bright " Loch Goil" dost stand,
With kindly, yet defiant brow,
    Fit homage to command.

Guarding her maiden beauty's pride
    In thy calm majesty—
How oft I long'd to climb thy side
    In happy days gone by !
Still may thy waterfalls rush free,
    Thy sweet-gale* scent the air !
My blessing, giant friend ! on thee
    And on thy sister fair !

* " Sweet gale " or " Bog-myrtle," deliciously aromatic.

LOCH GOIL BY MOONLIGHT.

THE lake was sleeping calmly bright,
  Beneath the Summer moon ;
E'en lovelier in that chastened light,
  Than in the blaze of noon !
And, as admiringly we dwelt,
  On the sweet moonlit scene—
Both voices cried—as *both hearts felt*—
  " I would he here had been ! "

The soft breeze teemed with odorous bloom,
  The lime's delicious flower ;
While the dark mountains' solemn gloom
  Half awed us in their power.
As in that sweet enchanted air
  My soul exulted free,
Methought, " if *Earth* has scenes so fair,
  " *Oh ! what must Heaven be ?* "

What must it be ? *so vainly* here,
  May yearning Nature try
To realise some faint idea
  Of blest Eternity !
No pain ! *No tears !* *No* parting woe !
  All sin to be forgiven !
E'en *deeper*, purer love to know !
  Thus it will be in Heaven !

Once more to meet those " *Gone before* "
  Their crown of faith to win !
Through those bright gates thus evermore,
  May we all enter in !

When Earth's fond ties are rent apart,
   May angels' sheltering wings
Bear unto Christ each trembling heart
   Unto the Cross which clings!

For still, while sojourners below,
   Each their own cross must bear;
And only *One above can* know,
   How sore our burdens are.
He gives us blessings numberless,
   And mercy—brightest gem—
Shines like a star when sins oppress,
   Though all the world condemn!

O Thou! Who thus beneficent
   Dost shower Thy good gifts still;
Teach me the lesson of content,
   Whatever be Thy will!
Teach me, whilst rich in health and love
   (Those best boons to us given),
Ne'er to forget our home above
   But lift my thoughts to Heaven!

                                 August, 1855.

ADIEU, LOCH GOIL!

ADIEU, Loch Goil! Thou beauteous lake!
   Full many an eye may gaze,
Full many a lip sweet verses make,
   Enamoured—in thy praise!
But never fonder heart will beat,
   Borne o'er those waves of thine;
Nor records bear away, replete,
   With richer store *than mine!*
     *   *   *

In *Sorrow's* hour thy stormy swell
    Responsive murmurs gave ;
And plaintively sighed forth a knell,
    For dear ones in the grave.
But oh ! When *Love and Joy's sweet dream*
    Made all this Earth their own ;
Then did thy flashing ripples seem
    To give an answering tone.

       *   *   *

Adieu, Loch Goil ! It matters not
    Thy sisters claim the palm—
And *Lomond's* charms are not forgot—
    But memory shall embalm
Within her choicest casket still,
    And keep *thee* aye in view ;
Farewell to river and to hill !
    To thy *wild shores*—Adieu !

                                     May, 1856.

GEM OF THE HIGHLANDS.

(*On revisiting Loch Goil after Ten Years' absence.*)

ONCE more, lovely Lake ! wafted o'er thy blue water,
Amid the grand mountains, serenely enshrined ;
Methought, of all exquisite objects in nature,
None e'er could compete with *thy* charms in my mind.
Beautiful ! Beautiful ! hallow'd by memory !
Was it not joy o'er that bright lake to glide ?
With Friends, whose young bosoms thrill'd deep in
    their ecstacy,
And *He ! that "Beloved One,"* close by my side !

Ben Donich smiled soft in the sunshine resplendent;
Ben Viula blushed rosy in Autumn's rich glow;
The woods of Drimsynie   breathed welcome most
    eloquent;
"Oh! why did ye leave us? Oh! why did ye go?"
Long years have elapsed, since we dwelt in our
    Highland home,
Silent and sure old Time's changes speed on;
But cold as yon rock must this warm heart in death
    become,
Ere it forget the blest days that are gone!

Drimsynie! though strangers by lawful right own ye,
How oft in my dreams to your scenes I repair!
Again through your wild glen I wander delightedly,
Gathering fern leaves and flowers so fair!
Ah! was it not sweet, as I roved in the dingle,
To hear, 'midst the plash of the oars on the sea,
A bugle-note often at even-tide mingle,
Sure herald of love and home gladness to me?

There was not a peak of the mountains surrounding,
Where, of yore, I have watch'd the bold sportsmen
    ascend,
Nor a crag where the graceful fleet roe-deer were
    bounding,
Nor a bank by the river, that seem'd not my friend!
Beautiful! Beautiful! hallow'd by memory!
Full of remembrances, words may not tell;
To see thee once more in thy beauty enchanted me!
Gem of the Highlands!—I bid thee Farewell!

                       1865.

FLOWERS OF AUCHENGRAY.

Written from 1852 *to Novr.,* 1871.

FLOWERS OF AUCHENGRAY.

———◆———

INTRODUCTORY LINES.

O LOVELY Flowers! to Earth God's sweetest gift!
    Ye fill my heart with ever new delight ;
Oh! may ye oft my fancy Heaven-ward lift,
    And to pure grateful piety incite!
Fill me with yearnings for that brighter Home,
    Where spirits dwell in blissful fadeless bowers ;
Like them, hereafter, may I too become
    One of Eternity's unchanging Flowers!

———◆———

SCOTCH THISTLE.

" Nemo me impune lacessit !"

HAIL! Scotia's emblem! honest Thistle!
    Bravely blooming in the wind—
Touch her not rudely!—or each bristle
    Will resent the grasp unkind !
Hers is a Royal bounty !—careless !
    Freely scattering to the breeze,
Her plumed gifts—Dame Nature's " largesse "
    From her silver treasuries !

———◆———

"THE WHITE HEATHER."

Considered in the Highlands as the symbol of " Good Wishes" and "Good Luck."

LIKE snow wreaths upon the dark moorlands flung,
    When the hot sun of August is blazing on high ;

Or chaplets of seed pearl, by millions strung,
  The lovely "White Heather" salutes mine eye!
"*Prosperity's*" beautiful emblem—hail!
  Thou sweet, fair bride of the Purple Heath!
Still whisper on softly thy joyous tale!
  And "*Good Wishes*" convey with thy fragrant
    breath

THE HEATHER!
(A Song for the 12th of August.)

Oh! the Heather! the bonnie cheery Heather!
  Blooming o'er the wide empurpled moor!
Oh! the Heather! the bonnie fragrant Heather!
  Dearly do I love it! *Scotland's favourite flower!*

O'er thy tufts, the sportsman's step is springing,
  Where the grouse have claimed their own sweet
All in vain! aloft in flight they're winging,   [home,
  For to them, the hour of doom has come!

Sportsmen prize the simple odorous flowers;
  'Minding them of many a day's delight!
Wholesome toil, and friendship's social hours,
  No exotics e'er seem to them so bright!

Hark! amidst the ferns and bluebells humming,
  Roving bees collect their honeyed store;
Until weary of the task becoming,
  Evening warns the labourers to give o'er!

Crowning the hills with a rich red glory,
  Fringing the streamlets down the rocks which flow,
Silent listeners to each sportsman's story,
  Flourish on, sweet heather! in thine Autumn glow!

·THE LADY'S MANTLE.

THE Lady's Mantle gracefully
 Unfolds her emerald robe so neat —
Ah! vainly may our fashions try
 With such apparel to compete!
Those tiny fringes! (trim device!)
 That well cut " Cloak or Overall,"
Is Queen Titania's, when the ice
 Lies thick upon her banquet-hall!

———◆———

LINES.

OH! lovely flowers! beloved flowers,
 Ye have a wondrous might
To call back visions of past hours
 Of youth and beauty bright.
From earliest infancy till death,
 Wherever I may be,
Your beauteous hues, your perfumed breath,
 My fond delight will be!
Amidst God's mercies numberless,
 Adore the hand which gives
Sweet flowers to gladden and to bless
 Each grateful heart that lives!

———◆———

THE RAGGED ROBIN, OR WILD CLARKIA.

So hardy! and so rosy bright!
 Wild Clarkia! thou hast been
Always my special favourite
 Wherever thou wert seen.

Now blooming amongst the sedges,
   Close to forget-me-not ;
Now smiling in the hedges
   And gladdening each spot !
There grows no flower in dell or wood,
   But emblem seems to me
Of something that is fair and good,
   And breathes of sympathy.
With moral attributes of mind,
   Some kindred grace revealing ;
Yes ! each sweet blossom is entwined
   With memory and feeling !
The Ragged Robin modestly
   Her humble claim doth press,
And thus appears fit type to be
   Of *Sportive Cheerfulness !*

THE LADY RUSH.

Now, who has dared gather the Lady-Rush ?
   The soft feather couch of the Moorland Fairy ?
Whose delicate beauty can scarcely crush
   The down as she swings on these petals airy !
Oh ! sweet her repose 'mongst the heather bright,
   And the blue-bells trembling in balmy air ;
But the elves would be sure to wake up in a fright
   Did they know that a *mortal* had been there !
   *   *   *   *
Nay ; it is not safe, and 'tis very rude
   To be trespassing thus in the " Good Folks "
   home,
They might punish the bold feet which intrude
   On the spot, where at midnight they're wont to
   roam.

Am I not the gay fairy's sworn ally?
  Do you think she would harm her true lover?
    " hush!"
We've kept faith with each other right loyally,
  So I fear not to gather the Lady-Rush!

———◆———

THE WHITE HAREBELL.
(RELIGIEUSE DES CHAMPS—NUN OF THE FIELDS.)

NUN of the fields, so heavenly pure,
  Thy downcast beauty charms the eye.
In thy white innocence secure,
  Thou reck'st not that the butterfly
  Should (half contemptuous) pass thee by.

No! Like some vestal, meekly bright,
  Thy graceful head is pensive bent.
Let yon vain rover wing his flight!
  To be his toy thou art not meant.
  Smile on, smile on, in calm content!

Rejoice thou still, fair gentle flower:
  In the glad sun and breezes free,
Live on serenely! Hour by hour,
  Emblem of sweet simplicity,
  And of unsullied thoughts to me!

———◆———

THE SILVER LEAF.
(GATHERED IN SEPTEMBER.)

WHAT shining gems upon the ground
Are these, which 'mongst the grass I've found?
The lovely little leaves! which spread
A covering o'er earth's dying bed,

Like frosted silver, kindly stay,
When summer friends have passed away.
*   *   *   *
Its golden bloom—gone long ago—
You'd scarce from yellow cistus know ;
But 'mongst the flowers of August bright
Doth often fascinate the sight.
But though it richly gilded be,
The *silver* leaf most pleases me !

THE GRASS OF PARNASSUS.

GRASS of Parnassus ! on dear Scotia's hills,
Cheer'd by the music of a thousand rills,
        Thine ivory cup expands !
That golden disc, which glitters in the sun,
Perchance thy classic reputation won
        In southern lands !
But *never* canst thou look more fair to me
Than when, exulting in the breezes free,
        I see thee bloom
Amongst the rocky paths and solitudes,
Where no invading city crowd intrudes
        On thy wild home.

WHITE CUDWEED.
(IMMORTELLE.)

WHITE Cudweed, with her face so fair,
Springs up in autumn here and there,
A mournful emblem, linked with Death !
    For often on some loved one's tomb
The mourner hangs its lasting wreath—
    A type of memory's fadeless bloom !

ON SOME SEA-WEEDS

Brought from the Ayrshire Coast by dear Lady Mary.

'TIS not the value of the thing we give ;
  It is the thought in absence which we prize—
The sympathy that bids remembrance live :
  The wish to be together it implies.

And thus a weed, a pebble, or a flower,
  With blest significance may be endued,
To soothe the aching heart in sorrow's hour,
  Or add a double zest in joy's bright mood.

———◆———

THE ST. JOHN'S WORT,

OR DWARF HYPERICUM.

I JOY to see thee, bright Hypericum,
  With thy sweet tiny buds of burnished gold ;
Exhaling forth an aromatic gum
  Of odour resinous. On moor and wold
I often find the flower of Saint John   [ing ;
  Amongst the prickly whins and furze-brake peep-
Always so fresh and gay to look upon,
  And long its brilliant hues untarnished keeping.

*   *   *   *

The large varieties in hedgerows dwell ;
  But most these little flowerets please mine eye,
For not too powerful the fragrant smell
  Which doth attract the wanderer passing by.
O beauteous nature ! with what endless charm
  Thou dost each sense enchant, each thought be-
The coldest heart thy loveliness must warm, [guile ;
  The dullest fancy glow beneath thy smile !

THE WOOD-SAGE.

(TEUCRIUM SCORODINIA.)

THERE'S not the simplest flower or weed
　　But has some virtue here ;
From Wood-Sage oft the peasant Swede,
　　Improves his home-brew'd beer !
Its little spike of greenish white
　　And wrinkled leaflets brown,
Though lacking beauty rare and bright,
　　A pleasant fragrance own.

———◆———

ON SOME WILD FLOWERS GATHERED BY SIR A. AND LADY G.

SWEET records! lie there of a happy re-union ;
　　Flowers culled by dear hands lately clasped in fare-
　　　　well!
Memorials of lively, delightful communion,
　　Of festive enjoyment and pleasure ye tell :
But chiefly of friendship! a friendship unchanging,
　　In joy and in sorrow through many a year :
So while these mixed leaves I am deftly arranging,
　　I look on the page with a smile and a tear.
　　　　　　　　　　　　. *Auchengray, Oct.,* 1870.

———◆———

BALM-WOOD FIG-WORT.

(SCROPHULARIA SCORODORINA.)

No herb that grows, no plant that springs
　　Without some destined good ;
How wonderful ! all earthly things
　　Are with a gift endued.

This plant is rich in healing power,
   Its worth I well can prove ;
Oh! how the plants and flowers each hour
   Tell of our Maker's love!

GOLDEN ROD ; OR, SUMMER FAREWELL.

(SOLIDAGO VIGAUREA.)*

"SUMMER FAREWELL" old custom styles
   This lovely flower of golden hue ;
But, as it in November smiles,
   T'were fitter "*Autumn's last Adieu!*"

FROZEN FERN LEAVES.

THE white hoar-frost lay heavy
   O'er hill, and wood, and dell,
The lovely Ferns looked dreary
   Beneath that wintry spell.
Though bright the silver glisten'd
   On blade, and leaf, and spray,
I paus'd awhile—and listen'd
   To what the Ferns would say.
     *   *   *   *

"Frost King, we humbly render
   The homage all thy due !
But oh ! this icy splendour
   Doth chill us through and through.
We love the sunbeams cheery,
   The soft refreshing rain,
But oh ! these diamonds weary—
   These jewels give us pain !"
     *   *   *   *

* This flower grows wild in Inverary.

D

Thus fainting, sad, and sighing,
  Their graceful heads bent down,
The pretty ferns lay dying
  Beneath the Ice-King's frown.
E'en thus, methought, the glitter
  Of pomp and luxury,
To fond hearts doth grow bitter,
  When love's glow hath gone by !

WILD BOUQUET.

. (GATHERED BY THE LADY, M. T.)

DEAR little Flowers, ye will be cherish'd
  Long after time has wither'd ye ;
Yes ! when each lingering tint has perish'd,
  Lovely to heart and memory.
The records of our woodland walk,
  Of quickly fleeting, happy hours,
Sweet gentle words, and friendly talk,
  Ye bear a charm in ye—Wild Flowers !
But chiefly, that from earth removed,
  These Autumn Blooms were cull'd for me,
By a white hand so fondly loved—
  So treasures they will ever be !

Sept. 1868.

EPILOBIUM OR WILLOW HERB.

THERE seems to be High Festival
  In Flora's court to day ;
The Bees are holding Carnival
  Amongst these flowers so gay.

Of exquisite Magenta
  With spikes of deeper hue,
Within each roseate centre
  Some Reveller lies *perdu !*

A happy hum betrays them,
  Their Bacchanalian strain—
Where on each fragrant bosom,
  The little rogues have lain !

Oh ! what a store of treasure
  They have been getting there !
But envy not their pleasure,
  We too shall have our share.

The splendid Epilobium,
  (As Willow Herb known best,)
Requires no eulogium
  To have its charms confess'd.

And when those charms have past away,
  Soft feathery darts are shed
Like thistle-down in white array,
  To make the Fairie's bed.

———•———

THE FOXGLOVE'S BRIDAL.
The Red and White Digitalis.

HARK ! the Foxgloves' chimes are ringing,
  Ringing merrily in the air ;
" Come, sweet flowers," they're gaily singing,
  Come to the wedding of your Sister fair !
All in white—dressed for the bridal,
  See ! she bends her modest head—
She need fear no lovelier rival
  With her stately bridegroom red !

All the guests are flocking—jubilant
    To the Foxglove's wedding gay ;
While his sentries, tall and vigilant,
    Watchful, guard the bright array.
Beetles in their varnish'd panoply,
    Butterflies in spangled pride ;
All the best of insect chivalry
    Pay their homage to the bride.

Ladybirds in corselets shining,
    Moths with gold dust richly fleck'd,
Every softest tint combining,
    Hasten in their best robes decked ;
While the Harebells meekly mingle
    Their low music in the peal,
And each flower in wood or dingle
    Answers to the glad appeal.

ON ANOTHER VISIT.

(*Wild Nosegay gatherd by " The Lady Mary."*)

OH ! weary, weary world were this
    The only state we're doom'd to know !
Our shadowy gleams of fancied bliss
    Unrealised while here below !
Yet there are hours when spirits meet,
    From worldly cankering influence free—
Hours of communion, calm and sweet—
    And such, dear Friend, I owe to thee !
*   *   *   *
For many a year ! and oh ! how much
    Of happiness we two have shared ;
Though sorrow with its blighting touch,
    Has sometimes, hoped for joys impair'd !

These flowers cull'd by thine hand so soft,
Records of friendship deep and dear ;
Will sweetly whisper to me oft,
" *She will return to us next year.*"

Auchengray, Sept. 1870.

WILD BOUQUET.

(*Third and last gathered by the same hand at "Auchengray."*)

THE last Wild Flowers she gather'd there—
The last " home stroll " we took ;
True Friend in Hope—in Joy—Despair !
In ALL this heart can brook !
Ah ! not alone for *this* frail world,
Are such affections given ;
Love's wings, on Earth so often furl'd,
Will wide expand in Heaven !

Sept. 26*th*, 1871.

THE SEA PINK, OR THRIFT.

DEAR little Thrift ! thou mindest me
Of happy years long past ;
My Highland life, so sweet and free !
Those days which flew so fast
Amidst the mountains of Argyle—
My wild, romantic home !
Where Nature wore her summer smile,
And I so loved to roam !

* * * *

How oft I watch'd its roseate pride,
By the salt waves submerged ;
And then again, at ebb of tide,
The pretty flowers emerged

All glistening from the briny wave,
    Ev'n sweeter than before ;
Loch Goil had deign'd their bloom to lave
    Upon the sandy shore.

Long ere the sun those tufts could dry,
    The busy bees would come ;
Sing to their friends caressingly,
    And carry largess home.
I never mark the sweet Sea Pink
    In garden borders grow,
But of that lovely lake I think,
    And the dear "long ago ! "

Again Ben Donich's giant form
    Seems towering above ;
While on the lake, in calm or storm,
    The graceful vessels move.
Again I hear the eagle's cry,
    And watch the roe deer flee !
Lovely Loch Goil ! how tenderly
    Remembrance clings to thee !

———◆———

SNOWDROP, or GALANTHUS.

FAIR Virgin Flower ! Spring's earliest harbinger,
    Winter's pet child, we warmly welco.ne thee ;
Like angels' tears congealed, bright messenger,
    From purer spirit-land thou seem'st to me.
How lovely ! when in million clusters growing
    Deep in our woods, I see thee meekly shine ;
Or, on some high green bank serenely blowing,

What pleasure to climb up and make thee mine.
The "Flower of Milk"* thus doth thy name
    import—
But when we peep beneath thy drooping face
Green arabesques, as if in Nature's sport,
    Upon its ivory whiteness we may trace.
In Nature's sport? Ah, no! the hand Divine,
    Which hath created worlds and placed us here,
Disdained not to invest these leaves of thine
    With beauty that doth charm us year by year.

———◆———

FERNS COVERED WITH ICE AND HOAR FROST.

FROM the windows of my Scottish home,
    O'er the pine woods, where the hoar-frost lies,
I gazed—and I wished my feet could roam;
    But Old Winter looked in with his stony eyes,
And he froze up my body—but not my soul!
    Ah no! for with one elastic bound
I escaped from the despot's stern control,
    And sensations of joy and peace I found.

      *   *   *   *   *

Great God! how beautiful Thy works!
    The frost, and the ice, and the snow praise Thee,
If a sinful thought in the bosom lurks
    'Tis rebuked by the sight of this purity.
The white, white world, shining all around
    (Emblematic of angels undefiled),
The grandeur and silence all around
    Make me feel like a spirit—or a child.

    * "Galanthus," meaning Flower of Milk.

A young bright form (which is near me now)
  To the lake midst the brackens, had swiftly flown,
With the wild deer's speed, and returned in a glow,
  With these fern leaves all with diamonds strewn.
The frost had bedeck'd them with crystals bright,
  Though embrown'd by age and the wintry blast.
I prize them—and feel they will bring to my sight
  Sweet visions of home, which for ever last !

February, 1870.

TO HEATHCOTE.

THE Wintry morn was dark and chill,
  As through the woods we stroll'd,
Yet Autumn beauty linger'd still
  Amid her leaves of gold.
The lovely ferns, all trail'd along,
  Lay drooping 'neath our feet,
While Robin Redbreast's cheery song
  Resounded, clear and sweet !
You talk'd of India's fervid clime,
  Of joys and perils past :
The changes made by death and time
  Since we two had met last—
And oft recurred one cherish'd name
  Which bore in all a part.
Yes ; ever to our lips it came,
  As ever in our heart.

*   *   *   *

Ah, dear one ! may that memory,
  So sacred and so deep,
That name we utter lovingly,
  Thy life from error keep.

The path of honour still be thine—
The path thy father trod—
Enlighten'd by the love Divine
Which guards the Child of God !

THE FORGET-ME-NOT BED AT AUCHENGRAY.

*The Burial Place of my little King Charles Spaniel " Tiny " (in 1862),
dear little Skye Terrier " Spur " (1870), and my Bullfinch (1871).*

DEAR little favourites ! here—one by one—
  With many a sigh your poor remains were laid,
Your warm, true hearts are cold, your duty done,
  Your happy gambols o'er, your moan is made.
Beautiful " Tiny !"   Darling, honest " Spur !"
  And " Bully," with his shining velvet crest !
Alas ! your mistress has no power to stir
  Those still limbs now—for ever they're at rest.
Sleep on beneath the blue " Forget-me-not ;"
  Your lives cheer'd mine, dear faithful little pets !
Fond memory hovers round your burial spot,
  The friend who cherish'd ye, not one forgets.

MINNIE'S WILD BOUQUET.

A CLUSTER of sweet native flowers,
  Brought by a fairer flower to me ;
Their fate to bloom a few short hours ;
  Hers, destined for eternity !

Oh joy, to be at home again,
  To breathe dear Scotland's healthful air !
And throw aside the weary chain
  Of worldly ways and fashion's glare.

I'd rather pass my days among
    These wild fresh hills by the lake-side ;
Than shine the envied of a throng
    Who sacrifice to pomp and pride !

Though pleasure's cup awhile may tempt,
    In gayer scenes and courtly hall,
Satiety soon brings contempt ;
    But Nature's charms can never pall !

No, never ! to the Good and True—
    No, never ! to the thoughtful mind !
Which traces in each drop of dew
    The love of God to all mankind.

Sweet flowers ! ye teach the self-same tale,
    Lifting your bright heads to the sky ;
Your grateful fragrance ye exhale,
    Still looking heavenwards till ye die.

Ah ! let these lovely monitors,
    Dear Minnie, not unheeded be ;
Referring all to one " First Cause,"
    Sweeter each gift to thee and me.

July, 1871.

IN RICORDANZA.

(*Poor little faithful " Spur's" Last Walk with me in the Auchengray Woods.*)

THOSE lovely Summer days of calm delight !
    How sweet to rove amongst the woods for hours,
Gathering the cool dark ferns and heather bright,
    With little " Spur " * careering o'er the flowers !

* " Spur," the most faithful of Skye Terriers.

Ah! little did I think, that glorious day,
  As, vauntingly, the leafy prize he bore,
How soon his simple joys would pass away,
  And all our happy sylvan walks be o'er!

    *   *   *   *

Dear little Spur! type of Fidelity!
  No tongue—no pen my fond regret can tell;
But many a tear deplores thee silently,
  And memory lingers o'er our last farewell.

FLOWERS BY THE LAKE.

By the lake side, sweet Auchengray,
How oft t'was my delight to stray!
And on the wild and varied ground
How many a floral gem I found!
Marigold, thyme, and marjoram,
And "lady's mantle" close to them;
Whilst, high above the dark pine wood,
Disturber of its solitude,
The heron spread his wings to soar,
Or circled round the fern-clad shore.
The fish leapt in the water bright,
Unconscious of the foe in sight;
And on mine ear the drowsy hum
Of happy insect life would come.
On the green bank t'was sweet to lie
Beneath the azure Summer sky!
Thanking my God, Who made the scene
For those long hours of joy serene;
Too calm! too free from care to last!
Sad heart! be grateful for the past!

JUNE THOUGHTS.

(MINNIE'S SONG.)

I RECLINE on this bank of pansies,
   Looking up to the Summer sky,
While a myriad of pensive fancies
   Bring tears—sad tears to mine eye!
I think of my hopes departed ;
   Of the fading joys of youth ;
Of those who have proved false-hearted ;
   Of fond vows which spoke no truth!
O weary world! Is it ever so?
Come, Hope, bright angel, and tell me No ! "

I think of the sweet wild wishes,
   Which fill'd my aspiring breast ;
How I long'd for the power which riches
   Would bring to make others blest !
Bright visions of love and beauty
   Ere a blight fell on life's first bloom,
'Tis a cruel change—but duty
   Forbids this desponding gloom.
Sweet angel Hope! Must it aye be so ?
She whispers—" On Earth—but in Heaven, No."

E'en here—though the deepest sorrow
   Thy wounded bosom cleave ;
Though grief and misfortune harrow,
   And the trusted may deceive ;
There is balm for the stricken spirit,
   And a noble aim for thee,

In the gift which we all inherit,
  Work for Eternity !
Sweet angel Hope! it is ever so?
"Change is for Earth—but in Heaven—No."

If Faith but unlock the portals
  Of mind to congenial mind,
How oft with our fellow mortals
  True sympathy we find!
Then say not that "Life is weary;"
  That we suffer "the more we love;"
When this varying world seems dreary,
  Let us look up to Heaven above!
Sweet angel Hope! It is even so!
Shall I yield then to Sadness? "No! ah! No."

                              June, 1866.

———◆———

TO JAMES B——, ESQ.

In the 17th year of our Acquaintance and Friendship.

FLED! like the wind, has many a year
  Since first we saw each other;
And Time still renders trust more dear,
  And makes thee more a brother.
For many a year beneath our roof
  Thy step has come and gone;
Trouble has ne'er kept thee aloof,
  Nor slander changed thy tone!

T'was first our Highland hills among
  You learnt our joys to share;
When sport by day, and nightly song,
  Defied the frown of care.

Ever from my "beloved one"
  A welcome did'st thou meet;
No warmer, heartier benison,
  A faithful friend could greet!

Oft, side by side, ye sallied forth
  To hunt the graceful roe;
Braving the keen breeze of the North
  Amidst the frost and snow.
Oh! beauteous lake! enchanting scene!
  Loch Goil's romantic shore—
I love to think on what HAS BEEN,
  Though it can be no more.

I bade thee gather leaves and flowers
  To ornament my page;
Fit emblems of the sunny hours
  Which gild our pilgrimage.
And, 'mongst the boons of purest worth,
  To us poor mortals given,
Is friendship! which, begun on earth,
  Will bloom (we trust) in Heaven!

December, 1870.

THE ALPINE WALK.

O BRIGHT sweet Morn! as through the wood
  There wander'd blithe and gay
A band of friends, in sportive mood,
  From dear old Auchengray.
Two graceful sisters, stalwart Fred,
  Flirt, Spur, and Minnie bright;
All by their loving hostess led
  To climb her "Alpine height;"

What merry jests—what mimic fears—
    With silvery laughter heard!
Fond memory each sound endears—
    Repeats each careless word.
The Forest boughs we had to part—
    The leaps o'er bank and burn—
Ah! never more to ONE sad heart
    Can such a day return.

The brown Scotch moors, so wild and free!
    Close to those sylvan bowers,
The dogs (dear faithful pets!) whose glee
    Quite emulated ours.
While to *mine* ear the ringing voice
    Of a *loved* sportsman nigh,
Made every bounding pulse rejoice—
    Oh! happy time, gone by.

Though late the season, blooming still
    The waving ferns among,
Were blue-bells, heather, Tormentil ;
    And oft sweet bursts of song
From gentle Sally filled the glen,
    As, roaming here and there,
She cull'd some floral specimen,
    And treasured it with care.

That Alpine Walk with zig-zag stair,
    Where Bessie faltering, paused,
One little foot poised high in air—
    The saucy laugh it caused.
As Fred his kind broad shoulder lent,
    And onward they progress'd
So grandly in their steep descent,
    This sketch will take the rest!

This pretty picture—flower enframed,
   I gaze on lovingly!
Time was a smile alone it claim'd,
   But now—it wakes a sigh.
Since! oh, what grief has cast its shade,
   And joy has bade farewell ;
Yet memory can never fade,
   Nor lose its soothing spell !

> *Our Walk, November 6th,* 1869.
> *My record of it written February,* 1872.

THE LAST FLOWERS GATHER'D IN MY SCOTTISH HOME.

November 13, 1871.

THESE faded flowers, so bright of yore,
   Are emblems of my fate !
Joys that once bloom'd, to bloom no more,
   Wither'd, and desolate !
My life lies wasting 'neath the touch
   Of one consuming fear ;
Terror ! for him I love so much ;
   Dread ! lest cold death be near.
Oh Thou ! on whom alone our hearts
   Can lay their heavy care,
Have mercy on the wound that smarts ;
   Oh, Heavenly Father—spare !

MISCELLANEOUS POEMS.

E

MISCELLANEOUS POEMS.

FAIRLIGHT GLEN.

SWEET Fairlight Glen! in thy deep recess,
Where a thousand varied beauties dwell,
How we pilfer'd thy flowery wilderness
As we bent our steps to the Dripping Well.
The treasures we gather'd! how fresh and bright
Look'd those buds and bells on thy banks so high!
Loveliest—half-conceal'd from sight
By the reeds, as the stream went rippling by.
Oh! surely the dryads themselves have made
Their favorite home 'neath the beechen shade,
O'erhanging the basin in that green dell
Which woodland spirits throne?   Oh, tell!
The twisted roots of that ancient tree
Are the nightly haunt of Titania's train,
And its boughs form their glorious canopy.
Hark! hark! to the nightingale's song again,
What wonder she loves to linger here,
Where the rivulet flows on so fresh and clear
Ere 'tis gathered into the silent pool,
Where the deer-grass dips its long leaves so cool,
And the bright cup-moss, like a wreath of gems,
Crowns the water with its diadems?
What marvel she gives her minstrelsy
To the woods midst such lovely scenery?

Could ye not listen for ever, now—
As, hid 'mongst the tufts of the chestnut bough
She pours forth that wild enchanting lay,
Stealing the cares from our hearts away ?
Care ! name it not in a spot like this,
While we're breathing an atmosphere of bliss.
Nature's own beautiful *spells* shall bind
Their welcome chain on the willing mind :
And if there be sorrow in bosoms here
Let her soothing magic that grief endear !

   * * * * *

But, wend we on ! and with climbing feet
Seek we the far-famed Lover's Seat,
Ere we reach the cliff through the deep woods till,
We ascend, to surmount the toilsome hill,
Where the pale primrose and yellow broom,
The golden furze with its fragrant bloom,
The blue-bell and pink campanula,
And meek anemone's silver star
All tempt our uncertain steps to rove
From the path in search of the sweets we love.

   * * * * *

But now, when the steepest point we gain,
Oh, who would look back to the woods again ?
Ocean lies stretch'd 'neath the precipice ; `
Couldst thou fancy a scene more wild than this ?
The tall, dark cliffs, and the boundless sea,
Whose mighty waves, like war horses free,
Bound on, unrestrain'd by men's slight power ?
Is not this a romantic trysting bower ?—

A few steps lead to its rocky site,
Perch'd on a fearful dizzy height,
Whence the long descent leads down to the shore,
There the " Two " met who can meet no more !

　　　*　　*　　*　　*　　*

T'was mournful! that young pair's history :
When dark frown'd the world on their destiny,
And their plighted troth was held false and light,
She met him here, in the silent night,
And her sailor love in his strong arms bore
His affianced bride to the friendly shore !
Oh, joy! midst the brightly glittering spray,
Their boat waits her coming—they are away !
Away from the cold and cruel hearts
Which know not the bliss that true love imparts,
Nor how easy to bear are all earthly woes
When the spirit in such trust may repose !
A brief space they were blest—alas !
Too swiftly do years of happiness pass.
Oft did she gaze on the restless deep
With a grateful thrill from her bower steep,
Recalling that evening so fraught with fear
When her sailor sought for and found her here.

　　　*　　*　　*　　*　　*

But one sad night, when the sky was dark,
He was out at sea in his slender bark,
She, watching its course—and while gazing on,
The moon peep'd, and show'd it—then, then 'twas
　　gone !
Gone with the treasure of life and soul !
O'er his lifeless corpse the billows roll ;

Gone! all that made existence worth,
In a moment's space—such her fate on earth!

    *   *   *   *   *

Sweet Fairlight Glen, and woods and well,
And " Lover's Seat," we must take farewell
Of your bright enchantments with regret,
But ye shall live in our memories yet?
Oh! as we linger'd around each spot
Was there one absent remember'd not?
Did we not wish in our hearts for some
Who might by kind fairy influence come
To share in the dreamy joy which thrill'd
Our bosoms? With Nature's rare beauty fill'd!
Did we not often and often say
" Oh, would they were with us! the far away."

    *   *   * · *   *

I NEVER felt the magic sense,
    Of beauty all my thoughts enthrall,
Nor bow'd to Nature's eloquence,
    But those best loved it did recall.
I never stoop'd to pick a flower
    But that its native sweetness spoke
To me of some past happy hour,
    And memories of a friend awoke!
Too oft, some little token bears
    A mournful message unto me,
E'en from the tomb—and sorrow tears
    The soft veil worn by memory.
But oh! it is a precious thing
    To feel that by this mystic power
Spirit to spirit still may cling
    In absence, through each parted hour.

To think that e'en a violet!—
   A lowly blossom may remind
The dearly-loved and absent yet
   Of one with happy hopes entwin'd.
The summer insect's busy hum,
   The flute-like notes of forest bird—
Nature to me is never dumb,
   But still by recollection stirr'd.
And I would have it thus with all
   Who wear my name within their heart,
For, let what may in life befall,
   That name in all would bear its part!

LINES

SUGGESTED BY THE MASSACRE AT HAUGO HEAD, AND THE
GALLANT CAPTAIN NEWMAN HALL'S FUNERAL TRIBUTE TO
THE VICTIMS IN 1855.

"HAUGO!" accursed shalt thou ever be
In blackest page of Russian history.
Lost to humanity, and dead to shame,
A brand is set on thy assassin name,
And Men hereafter when they speak of "treachery"
Shall cry, "a Haugo deed!" *if* vile enough it be.

And was it fit, unmourned our countrymen
Should meet their doom in that base coward's den?
When on sweet mercy's trusting errand sent
The "Cossack's" crew, unarmed, defenceless went,
Bringing the Finnish captain to his mother land,
His wife and children's home? Ah! dark, perfidious
    strand!

What greeting met they? From their ambush forth
Rushed the vile band—hyænas of the North :
And so they perished! while high Heaven looked
        down
And viewed the foul betrayal with a frown!
While false De Bergh, that wretch, with felon ribaldry
Laughed, as he saw the English dupes lured on to
        die.

But did I say unmourned they fell? Ah, no!
A nation's vengeance, and a nation's woe
Have made the " Savages " regret their crime,
And stigmatised them to the end of time ;
While Hall, chivalrous Hall, honour to him! has
        known
How to provide the victims with a burial stone!

Nor unrecorded was thy fate, fond wife!
Whose love and sorrow cut the thread of life,
" Sacred to those so barbarously slain—
" Sacred to her whose heart-strings burst with
        pain."
These words, upon a tablet reverently placed,
Never can be forgot—though soon, perchance,
        erased !

Now the procession, resolute and stern,
Armed to the teeth, to their own boats return ;
No flag of truce upheld by them I trow !
But in each breast lies registered a vow,
Wherever freedom's cause demands the righteous
        blow,
To strike for the betrayed, on bloody couch laid low.

Oh, sounder will ye sleep, ye true and brave !
Now friendly feet have trod your narrow grave :
Your gallant ocean brothers' manly woe,
Hallowed the spot which saw your life-blood flow,
Honour to him who caused the Holy Rites be said
Which living hearts console and consecrate the
    dead !

THE STRANGER'S ADIEU TO MORAY LAND.

(Written after a long and happy sojourn at Darnaway Castle, in 1839.)

FAREWELL ! a long and fond farewell, to thee, sweet
    Moray Land !
To thy wild rivers deep and clear—thine ocean-belted
    strand !
Green "Darnaway," whose forest leaves now wear
    their wintry hue,
With heavy heart the Stranger bids thy varied
    charms adieu !

"With heavy heart?" Ah, no ! by many a token
    prized and dear,
The thought of thee shall lighten care through every
    coming year ;
For, link'd with thy familiar name where Love with
    Beauty vies,
From their rich treasure caves shall still a thousand
    memories rise !

The "Findhorn's" sweeping waters, rolling on in
    kingly might ;
Now sleeping calm—now flashing by, in many a line
    of light ;

The giant rocks above them, which the cragsmen dare
    not scale,
Where the gnarled oak and Alpine fir sigh hoarsely
    in the gale.

The wild romantic banks, which fringe the winding
    Devy's side ;
The woodland paths, where bound the graceful roe-
    deer in their pride ;
The castles, where the Highland Chief now rules in
    peaceful power ;
All—all will ever present be, in Fancy's musing hour.

Too soon in Randolph's ancient hall the echoes mute
    will be,
Which late were wakened by the sound of festive
    mirth and glee ;
On Darnaway's high battlement the banner cease to
    wave ;
Which, free as flowed its silken folds, a generous wel-
    come gave !

The Stranger, who with lingering steps, must from the
    scenes depart,
Takes the lovely picture home in light and shadow to
    the heart ;
And with many a wishful look behind, as slow she
    waves her hand,
Sighs forth—"A long farewell to thee, thou bonny
    Moray Land !"

MORAY LAND.   '
(*Written in* 1846.)

O MORAY Land! sweet Moray Land! how often in
    my dreams
Thy varied scenery appears! the rapid Findhorn
    gleams
Athwart deep forest paths, and bright the mountain
    torrents fling
Their silvery wreaths of froth and foam like summer
    lightning.
I see the Earl's proud banners wave from battlement
    on high ;
I see the plaid I love so well—the Stuarts are passing
    by !
O Moray Land! dear Moray Land! my heart for joy
    would leap,
Could I but realise the dreams which haunt my trou-
    bled sleep !

Methinks I hear the bagpipe now as on that autumn
    day,
When with a band of cherish'd friends, with spirits
    light and gay,
We roved far in the forest depths ; whilst ever and
    anon
The sound of that wild minstrelsy beguiled our foot-
    steps on,
Through steep romantic winding ways, o'er precipice
    and flood,
Till on the heights, in frolic glee, the daring climbers
    stood.
We made the Forest echo, as we laughed so merrily !

O Moray Land! dear Moray Land! why are those
    days gone by?
I see Earl Randolph's hall decked out, as for a festal
    scene;
I see his high place fill'd by one whose countenance
    serene,
Whose kind and noble face beams forth with that
    benignant smile
Which welcomes all so graciously! his daughters fair
    the while
Presiding with a winning grace o'er that gay festival;
And all is joy and happiness within Lord Moray's
    hall.
And was I there?—I was.—Ah! would that with a
    fairy wand
I once more could re-visit thee, nor dream, dear Moray
    Land!

———•———

THE SHEPHERD'S CHIEF MOURNER.

(SUGGESTED BY SIR EDWIN LANDSEER'S BEAUTIFUL PICTURE.)

PART THE FIRST.

(*Representing the Dog Watching his Master's Coffin.*)

THE shepherd sleeps, he is at rest,
    And none are nigh to mourn the dead,
    Save one poor dog; whose faithful head
Against the coffin-lid is press'd!
See with what fond affection dwells
    His earnest gaze on that still thing!
Whilst a stray gleam of sunshine tells
    What nerved the parted spirit's wing—

The Book of Life! whose late-closed leaves
   With holy peace and comfort fraught,
   Were daily, humbly, meekly sought,
By him for whom yon mourner grieves.—
   Grieves with a deep intensity
   Which many a human heart might shame!
To change is *man's* propensity ;
   His love—too oft—not worth the name!

But thou, whose joy it was to wait
   On thy dear master's pleasure, still
   Tracking his steps o'er vale and hill,
Guarding his flock early and late !—
   Oh! would that *mortals* were as true,
   As thou, mute guardian friend, hast proved!
Oh! would that many a bosom knew
   What 'tis to love, as thou hast loved!

Behold, with what a piteous face
   He listens for one voice in vain!
   So late he watch'd his couch of pain!
He's gone from the accustom'd place ;—
Beneath the cruel boards they've hid
   That master's old and cherish'd form ;
And so he'll guard the coffin lid,
   Thinking—e'en there—his love may warm!

That humble, cheerless cottage room—
   The spectacles and vacant chair ;
   Though all deserted, bleak and bare,
A spell of beauty doth illume,
For He, who to yon fond brute gave
   Devotion past expression's power,
Vouchsafed a hope beyond the grave,
   To soothe the shepherd's dying hour!

PART THE SECOND.

*(Where he is represented standing close to his master's grave
in the country churchvard.)*

" DEAR faithful dog ! and art thou here again ?"
    Day after day still watching o'er his tomb,
Striving to pierce that grassy mound in vain
    As if thy love could see through Death's cold gloom.
Mark with what soft and almost stealthy tread
    He doth approach the green and daisied plot,
As if he feared to wake the silent dead
    Sleeping beneath the well-known hallowed spot.

Well known to him ! for, ever since the day
    Which saw his master to the churchyard borne,
Those faithful feet have tracked their constant way
    Whence never shall his shepherd friend return.
And oft he looks up to the village spire
    Remembering that mysterious funeral toll :
Fidelity ! such love thy depths inspire,
    We almost ask, Has thy dumb type *no soul ?*

———•———

SOLITARY MUSINGS.

ARE there not passages in life's rich page ?
    Are there not dangerous moments *"passing sweet,"*
Which bid us linger on our pilgrimage
    And try to stop the wheel of time ?   Our feet,
Our passive feet, must never know a rest,
    Borne down the pathway by resistless fate,
We've scarcely breath to own that we are blest,
    Ere sorrow and her train knock at our gate !

Too late we feel what *might* have made us rich
   In every joy our mental state can know ;
Too late ! we've peopled every secret niche
   Of fond remembrance with some self-sought woe.
Oh ! could we but recall the precious past,
   " *How different*," say we, our career had been !
'Tis thus we blindly argue to the last,
   Until death closes on our fitful scene.

There is no resting-place for us on earth !
   A trite remark, but oh most deeply true ;
For ever, from the moment of our birth,
   We've hurried on to something fresh and new.
How often are we tempted to exclaim
   "Give us a pause ! some breathing time to know
More of our happiness than the mere name,
   More resignation in the midst of woe !"

It cannot be !—for ever, fate impelled,
   Our steps are hurried to some distant goal ;
Thrice happy they, who not alone propelled,
   By impulse guided, take unto their soul
Those calm grand principles of sacred light,
   Our only safeguard in life's mystic way,
Which are a lamp of comfort in the night,
   Of sorrow—and a sun in joy's bright day !

THE BUTTERFLY AT SEA.

(A party engaged in a sailing excursion were surprised, at the distance of twelve miles from shore, by the appearance of a butterfly fluttering on the mast. The circumstance gave rise to the following lines.)

   BRIGHT winged and brilliant wanderer !
     Child of the ambient air !
   What makes thee here a sojourner
     Far from thy playmates fair ?

The dew is on the rose leaves yet,
   Thine own beloved rose ;
The tear of sorrow and regret
   Fly back to thy repose !
In her soft bosom thou should'st lie
   Safe from our chilling gale—
Unheeded, must her fragrant sigh
   Breathe forth its plaintive tale ?
The dawn beheld her blushing cheek
   Exulting in thy love,
What moved thee other joys to seek ?
   What taught thee thus to rove ?
Beautiful stranger ! wild and free,
   What seekest thou upon the sea ?

         *   *   *   *   *

Far, far away, o'er the dark blue wave
   The butterfly has come,
Where the truant may find a watery grave,
   Alas, for his flowery home !
Full many a weary mile there lies
   Between the mighty main,
And the scented shore where the sweet rose dies
   He never may reach again.
Yet onwards still on his airy track
   His pinions bear him free,
Nor dreams he once of turning back
   All weary though he be.
No perfumed blossoms are here to bloom,
   His gay familiar friends,
Yet still to encounter an unknown doom
   His aimless flight he wends.

Creature of sunshine! self-exiled thus
    From all which suits thee best,
Bear'st thou no warning sign to us
    Of our own heart's unrest?
Of the wayward spirit's reckless bent,
    So prone to pine and range?
Of thanklessness for the rich gifts sent,
    And the wild desire for change?
Of blessings contemn'd within our reach
    Which should be prized the most?
All this may yon fluttering insect teach,
    Oh, let not the type be lost!

*   *   *   *   *

But see! he alights on our friendly mast
    With his spent and toil-worn wings:
Our bark will speed over the wave as fast
    As the lone one which to it clings.
Let us waft him back to his favourite rose,
    So loved from her fragrant birth:
Let us waft him back to each flower that grows,
    Fair children of verdant earth!
There are garlands the watery depths beneath,
    Where the seaweeds are floating on,
But none boast the rich hues or scented breath
    Of the rose, his chosen one.
So ere the dark shadows close around,
    And the world is of light bereft,
Our wanderer his welcome may have found
    In the fairy bowers he left.—
And when discontent lures *our* hearts to roam
    Ah! well it were, could we

F

On the Spirit's wings be borne scatheless home
Like the butterfly at sea !

———•———

THE NIGHTINGALE IN THE ACACIA TREE.

A NIGHTINGALE was singing
In the white acacia tree ;
Her song through the woods was ringing
With the richest melody.
That bird's enchanting music brought
A host of dreams to me,
With tender, mournful musings fraught,
Too dear to memory !

And as I stood and listen'd
To the warbler's witching tone,
The flowers in the sunshine glisten'd
With a glory all their own !
Yet bitterly I could have wept
O'er hopes and joys gone by ;
For " loved ones " in the grave who slept,
But that *one* form was nigh !

One of that band whom household love
Of yore so firmly bound ;
And in the song which peal'd above
A soothing spell I found ;
It seem'd to breathe a warning tone
In its entrancing strain ;
" Mourn not o'er hope and brightness gone,
Prize that which doth remain ! "

THE LITTLE MINERS.

YE merry, happy children, who can play amongst the
  flowers,
And feel the sweet fresh air blow soft amid your
  balmy bowers ;
Think what a different lot is theirs who work beneath
  the soil,
Digging the riches of the earth, with ceaseless care
  and toil !

There's many a little miner who but seldom sees the
  sky,
Buried in gloomy chambers deep, his days and weeks
  pass by ;
So dull his destiny ! Oh, pray that heavenly light
  may break
On each young soul so precious ! for the dear
  Redeemer's sake !

Give to the Pitmen's little ones the key of happiness ;
That key which opes bright Wisdom's door, and
  makes privation less ;
And though no joy of sunshine or of flowers to them
  be given,
Pray, when their life's dark task is done, themselves
  may bloom in heaven !

FOREST SONG.

SPEED ! speed ! speed !
  To the forest depths with me ;
Where the wild bee sips from the lime tree's bough,
  And the air blows fresh and free !

There the spirit of joy shall touch thy brow,
    And its gifts shall descend on thee ;
Oh ! this is the loveliest season now,
    In our forest haunts to be !
        Speed ! speed ! speed !

Speed ! speed ! speed !
    To the woodlands, mount and ride ;
No more midst the city's glare delay,
    But come ! for in beauty's pride
The wild flowers are blooming sweet and gay ;
    The deer in their covert hide.
Let us watch the graceful fawns at play
    By their gentle mother's side.
        Speed ! speed ! speed !

Speed ! speed ! speed !
    To the forester's dear home ;
Where the old oak spreads his mighty arms
    Let us rest 'neath its verdant dome !
There the sun with a softer glory warms,
    As o'er hill and dale we roam ;
There Liberty breathes her thousand charms :
    To our sylvan shelter come !
        Speed ! speed ! speed !

SUMMER DAYS.

OH ! welcome is the Summer, when she comes in all
    her pride;
Reminding me of happy days, when we rode side by
    side

O'er the smooth elastic turf, as our good steeds flew
along,
While our hearts were full of pleasant thoughts—our
voices full of song!

O halcyon Time so exquisite, of early love and truth!
Each pulse leapt up in gladness at the trumpet call of
youth;
No sordid cares weighed on us—no sorrows long
oppressed;
But generous trust in others made a heaven in the
breast.

Those days of Prime, alas! are gone, and youth's
bright joys are fled;
Our gay companions all are changed, or numbered
with the dead;
Yet ever—as the Summer comes to flower, and leaf,
and tree,
Sweet memories of the olden time it doth revive in
me!

And though Life's brilliant sunshine in its dazzling
glory fades,
A chasten'd, softer light, perchance, its warning bloom
pervades;
For fond and tried affection with a tender eye surveys
The wreck of youth and beauty—not less dear than
" Summer days! "

———

GOD'S SUNSHINE.

THE cold, cold snow, like a funeral pall,
Doth enshroud the cottage and lordly hall;
But God's bright sunshine is over all!

The winter of woe to all hearts must come,
To the peasant's cot, and the noble's home—
God's sunshine lights hovel and lofty dome.

The summer of joy cheers each human breast !
And love makes the poor as the rich man blest :
Whilst the sun shines on, and loves no one best.

TO THE ROBIN.

DEAR little bird ! that lovingly dost linger
  Amid the winter's storm, our hearts to cheer !
Sweet robin ! January's favourite singer !
  Thou bring'st the kindest message of the year—
Fond words ! and wishes : with affection fraught,
  Our absent cherished ones are wont to send
By thee the welcome harbinger they're brought,—
  And " Robin redbreast " is the general friend !

YOUTHFUL MEMORIES :

(ADDRESSED TO AN OLD PLAYFELLOW.)

DOST thou remember that deep green dell,
Where the earliest primrose was wont to dwell ?
Where the violets in the soft moss hid,
Dried the tear-drops within each dewy lid !
Dost thou remember how blithe and gay
Were the hours we used to dream away,
As our light and slender limbs we laid
Under the graceful willow's shade ?
Bending our heads to the rippling stream,
Where the trout, for an instant, with silvery gleam,

Would leap to the surface so merrily !—
Ah ! why are those happy days gone by ?

*   *   *   *   *

Dost thou remember the deep delight
Which lent us wings, when the sun shone bright
As we flew to our haunt in the greenwood ? Then
Exploring each sweet sequestered glen,
And hailing with gay triumphant shout,
Each bud and bell fresh peeping out
From some warm and closely sheltered nook ;
Where no eyes but our own had been to look,
For the treasures of lovely, blooming Spring,
Which a message from Summer (bright Summer)
      bring ;
Bidding us greet her with joy and smiles,
When she comes to illumine our sea-girt Isles !

*   *   *   *   *

Dost thou remember the furtive gaze
We stole around, at the flickering blaze
Of the wandering gipsy's fire, betrayed
By the smoke curling up through the friendly
      shade ?
How the fortune-telling elves came round
At the chink of the silver's welcome sound !
With their wild, dark eyes, and tangled hair—
Yet with something of pride, in their Moorish air—
As if, in their strange and vagrant lot
Were a charm, which the world divineth not.
Dost remember the willing faith we lent
To the mysteries of their low, dark tent ?

While they talked of the stars which would rule our
    fate,
Dealing out honours, and wealth, and state?
How we listened with awe! and yet smilingly,
As they read the lines in our destiny!

       *   *   *   *   *

Oh! holiday period of happy youth,
When all sweet, bright visions looked like truth!
Oh! season of pleasure without alloy,
From the chill which impaireth all future joy:
That cold cloud which stern experience throws
O'er the warm sanguine bosom that fondly glows
With the light shed by hope in her fairy track!
Dear and vanished days! will ye ne'er come back?

       *   *   *   *   *

Ah, no! though the depths of the forest glade
Are as lovely as when of old we played
In their green recesses!—though fount and rill
Are sparkling and flowing like crystal still—
Though the fawn bounds along by its mother's side,
And the hares in their leafy covert hide—
Though the wilding rose blushes on, unseen,
And the soft grass is marked by those circlets
    green
Which show the night haunts of the elfin train,
When Titania gives way to her frolic vein—
Though all nature is blooming—as 'twas of yore,
Those enchanting days can return no more!

       *   *   *   *   *

Yet! come—come away : though long years have
    flown,

And thought, care, and sorrow their shade have
  thrown
O'er the features which shone once so radiantly
  glad—
Though the brow may be heavy—the glance may
  be sad,
There's a magic impression, a fresh breathing spell
In those scenes of our childhood we cherished so
  well.
Come away from the courtly, the formal, the vain,
'Twill revive thy worn heart to escape from their
  chain!
Early memories into thy breast shall steal,
And waken its depths with their soft appeal,
And the answer prove true to old sympathies yet,
Not "Dost thou remember?" but, "Can'st thou
  forget?"

WARNING.

AGATHA.

"There is an error in the labyrinth
Of woman's life, whence never step returns.

GIOVANNA.

Hath God said this?

AGATHA.

O Lady! Man hath said it.

GIOVANNA.

He built that labyrinth—he led that foot
Into it—and then left it. Shame upon him!"
  [*From Walter Savage Landor's Tragedy of " Fra Rupert."*]

WOMAN, guard well thy spotless fame,
  Woman, steel well thy tender heart;
For, if one blot but soil thy name,
  Then must thy peace of mind depart

For ever, yes, for ever!
He who has won thee, may awhile
  Cling to the wreck his love has made,
Endure the absence of thy smile,
  And fain would with his oaths persuade
    That he will alter never!
But, oh, be sure the hour will come
When the sharp pang will strike thee home,
And all thine art will be in vain
To rivet that delusive chain.
Thou shalt be fettered! ay! but he,
Thy lawless lover, will be free !
Oh agony! to think of all—
  All thou hast given up for him!
What bitter tears must mourn thy fall,
  What dark thoughts make thy beauty dim !
    Muse on, and tremble!
See'st thou yon brilliant butterfly?
  The soft bloom on its feathery wing?
A rude touch has confused each dye
  On its bruised pinion, ill-used thing!
    What does its fate resemble?
Thine, fond and fragile being, thine!
Left in thy day of shame to pine,
Afraid to lift thy voice in prayer,
Remorse is added to despair,
And many a weary hour must cast
Its deepening shadow o'er the past,
And many a wild sad tear must flow
When memory wakes her tale of woe,
And many a penalty atone
For that sweet dream for ever gone!

Go forth into the hollow world,
　　And wreath with smiles thy pensive face.
Grant that no lip in scorn be curled,
　　No eye to haunt thee with disgrace ;
Grant that no human heart save one
　　Be conscious of the hidden stain ;
No eye thy shrinking glance to shun ;
　　But, followed by a numerous train
Of friends and flatterers, who grace
　　The chambers of the gay and great,
Thou keep'st unscathed thy lofty place,
　　A sharer in their sunny state.
Yet moments there will surely be
　　When the dark shadow will grow deeper,
And, if thy memory be free
　　From pain, remorse will wake the sleeper !
Then, when o'erwearied, faint and lone
　　(Thine idolised one far from thee),
Thy thoughts their secret burthen own,
　　And thy head bows upon thy knee,—
Then, when the stifled sob shall force
　　Its long forbidden, smothered way,
And burning tears shall hold their course
　　Down cheeks which lately looked so gay ;
Oh ! surely even the sternest mood
　　Would speak some comfort to thee now,
To one so fondly, wildly wooed,
　　Sitting there with pale, altered brow,
Musing in hopeless keen regret
　　O'er innocent calm days departed ;
But clinging to the loved one yet,
　　Though he has made her—Broken-hearted !

PLEADING.

CONDEMN not thou the guilty one!
  For little can'st thou know
The arts, the wiles which have undone
  And brought her now so low!
In other days she may have been
  Lofty and pure like thee,
As innocent and bright of mien,
  From sinful thought as free.
But oh! what human eye can read
  The trials unconfessed?—
The tempting hours to sin which lead,
  And wreck the unguarded breast?
By slow degrees beguiled from truth,
  Dazzled, and led astray,—
What snares for beauty and for youth
  Beset the flowery way!
Then, oh, condemn not harshly thou
  The erring, fallen one,
Nor with a cold and haughty brow
  Her trembling footsteps shun;
But thank thy God thou hast been spared
  The fiery ordeal,
Which others have so largely shared,
  To stain thy spirit's weal!
Yes, lift thy grateful eyes to heaven
  And drop a pitying tear
For her who prays to be forgiven
  When no stern gaze is near;
No glance to crush her with its scorn
  When drooping, penitent,

And, in her bitterness forlorn,
  Her upward prayers are sent.
Be sure that error leads to woe !
  And many a dreary hour
Must follow the deceitful glow
  Of bliss in pleasure's bower.
Then do not add thy weight of blame
  To sink her shattered bark,
O'erladen with the heavy shame
  Which freights her shivered ark.
No peace, no soft serenity
  Can smooth her troubled wave.
Oh ! view her fate with lenity ;
  For only in the grave
Can that poor fallen one find rest,
  Or be by those forgiven,
Whose virtue dwells not in the breast,
  But owes its strength to heaven.

THOUGHTS

ON THE LAMENTED DEATH OF
THE RIGHT HON. LORD GEORGE BENTINCK.

Addressed to his favourite Sister, September, 1848.

A STAR has fallen, a brilliant light is gone
  Which shed the flash of genius o'er the earth,
And tears spring fast, and bitter is the moan
  In ducal halls for him of noble birth—
He who has carved unto himself a name
  Which will illumine future history,
Lost to us in the zenith of his fame,
  But ever dear to England's memory !

Yes, gentle mourner! in thy heavy woe
   A nation's sorrow fain would share with thee,
And none but kindred bosoms e'er can know
   How deep the measure of that grief must be.
'Tis long since first I saw him, yet that face
   With its most speaking and expressive gaze,
That sunny smile, and true patrician grace,
   No time can ever from my mind erase!

So like a poet's vision, that reality!
   Ah me! that genius, beauty, soul, should seem
But meant to prove of life the vanity:
   Existence seeming but a lovely dream!
Oh, gifted spirit! which, so nobly free
   From every meaner attribute did'st soar,
Well may they weep who loved and valued thee:
   Honour be to thy memory evermore!

Amidst the vulgar, mercenary herd,
   Seeking the viler interests of their kind,
How glorious to find a man whose word
   Followed the genuine impulse of his mind!   '
Foe to oppression! advocate of right!
   Protector of the wronged, the poor, and weak,
Ithuriel's spear shone in that glance so bright,
   And hypocrites shrunk back, when thou did'st
     speak.

Now mute for ever is that voice which breathed
   Integrity's pure accents undismayed,
Though fresh and blooming still the trophies wreathed
   Which at his feet admiring fame has laid.

The world its glittering tribute scarce had given
  To worth and talent all too lately known,
When that bright spirit from its home was riven—
  Ah no ! to heaven, its native home, 'tis flown !

HAGAR.

THE cruse was empty, and the food had gone
Provided for the wanderer and her son :
Death in the wilderness ! the desert wild
Seems doomed for them—poor Hagar and her child.
She sees the colour from his young cheek fade,
She casts him down beneath a date-tree's shade,
And with a breaking heart she moistens now,
With heavy tears, his parched and burning brow ;
Folds him with anguish in her fond embrace,
And gazes on his changed and pallid face.
His grasp around her neck becomes more faint,
He cannot hear the words of her complaint ;
The hapless exile, delicately bred,
The stricken flower bows its drooping head.
Can Hagar stay to watch him perish there ?
She, weeping, turns away in her despair.

* * * * *

Death is upon his closing eye,
  Death in each languid limb ;
"Ishmael ! I cannot see thee die,
  Oh Father ! succour him !
Thou who dost oft in mercy bend
  From Thine eternal throne :
Forsaken by each earthly friend,
  Oh, take us for Thine own."

* * * * *

Weep no more, Hagar! for thy prayer is heard,
Ishmael revives at the Almighty word.
See.! at the waving of an angel's wings,
A fountain in the sandy desert springs.
Bright hopes for future years an angel's voice
Predicts, and bids thy trembling heart rejoice!
Heaven breaks upon thee in the savage wild,
For God has heard, and gives thee back thy child!

SONGS.

THE world may think me lonely,
 But they little know the heart
Which for thee Beloved only
 . Thus has played its desperate part!
With thee, to love and cherish—
 With thee, to soothe and bless;
All other thoughts must perish
 In our tried devotedness!

  *   *   *   *   *

Were I by thee forsaken,
 No tear should mark the change—
My soul—by ruin shaken,
 Would leave thee free to range!
In deep seclusion hidden,
 My life away would pine;
Till by fond memories chidden,
 Thou'dst mourn for what *was thine!*

A MAY SONG.

"MERRILY THE SUNBEAM GLEAMETH."

MERRILY the sunbeam gleameth
   Through the forest shades, so warm and bright ;
Merrily its radiance streameth
   O'er the green-sward, in long lines of light !
How my heart with delight would be beating,
   Were some loved companion near !
All the loveliness of nature greeting,
   Which now wakes the pensive tear.
I'm longing but for one ! but for one only
   To respond to my yearning spirit's call ;
" *It never can be good to be lonely !* "
   Thus saith Nature's voice unto each and all.

Pleasantly the streamlet glideth
   Down her course through the deep and rocky glen,
Gracefully the woodbine hideth
   The tangled path to the fox's den !
While the birds high above are singing
   Their varied, triumphant lay—
And soft winds, on their wings are bringing
   All the odours of fragrant May ;
I'm longing but for one ! but for one only,
   To respond to my yearning spirit's call—
" *It never can be right to be lonely !* "
   Thus saith Nature's voice unto each and all !

Oh ! when the wintry storm is howling
   Through the shivering, leafless wood,

And the tempest dark is scowling—
  How dreary is solitude !
But companionship will brighten
  The cloudiest, most threatening hour,
And sweet sympathy can lighten
  Every burden 'neath stern sorrow's power !
I'm longing but for one, but for one only,
  To respond to my spirit's yearning call—
"*It never can be wise to be lonely!*"
  Thus saith Nature's voice unto each and all.

———◆———

A SONG.

"OH DEEM ME NOT SO WEAK AND VAIN."

OH ! deem me not so weak and vain,
  Oh ! think me not so frail—
That only flattery's honied strain
  To win me can avail !
I'd rather hear truth's faithful voice
  Howe'er severe it be,
Or saddening—than take the choice .
  'Twixt flatteries and thee !
Perhaps it seems temerity
  So openly to chide,
But love—in its sincerity—
  Doth conquer wounded pride.
I'd rather hear thy frank reproof,
  Whilst sitting by my side,
Than bear to see thee stand aloof,
  Though all should praise beside.
    *   *   *   *   *

Alas! 'tis true! I fear 'tis true,
　My heedless smile may seem
To challenge homage as its due,
　And flash with pleasure's beam!
I know my spirits, gay and light,
　Too often overleap
Their lawful bounds—too wildly bright!
　When prudence goes to sleep.
Not theirs, the safe and useful gift,
　To keep an even tone—
Expended—with too little thought—
　They dazzle—and are gone!
But, though the world's most bland caress,
　No lasting joy can bring
Thou by thy faithful tenderness
　Hast touched its secret spring!

A LIFE.

A SMILING dawn, a fervid noon
　'Neath passion's burning ray,
Whose fierce breath, like the wild simoom,
　Scorches sweet peace away;
An eve refreshed by Heaven's soft dew,
　Rain of regretful tears:
Too bitter! till the angels flew
　To soothe that sad soul's fears.
Angels of mercy and of Ruth,
　Each with a snow-white wand,
Waving around the band of truth,
　Making their wings expand

To guard, with softly-healing touch
   The drooping, stricken form
Of one who'd " loved and suffered much "
   Beneath Fate's pelting storm.

*   *   *   *   *

O Saviour Christ, Thou bad'st despair,
   From mortal bosoms flee ;
Teach us to cast on Thee our care,
   Whate'er that care may be !
Teach us to heed no worldly scorn,
   Nor sink beneath our doom,
(He never spurns the heart forlorn
   Nor leaves it to its gloom).

Inspire us with kind thoughts of all,
   And if by insult stung,
Bid us the hasty words recall
   Which hover on the tongue.
Ah yes ; withdraw thy gaze from earth,
   Look upward—look above !
And realise how little worth
   Is aught, save faith and love.

May, 1873.

MEDITATIONS IN ILLNESS.

THROUGH many a weary, lonely hour
   My mind has been oppressed
With thoughts of the Almighty power,
   Which give my heart no rest ;

Yet closer, firmer may I cling
    To Christ—to Him alone
Who can the lowest sinners bring
    Back to His Heavenly Throne.

Yes! even to one so lost as I,
    Who all through life have erred ;
Forgiveness He will not deny,
    As promised in His word !

Well may our trembling spirits yearn
    For pardon and for grace—
Oh, sweet to know He will not turn
    From contrite ones His face !

What though the cold world should desert,
    And fondest love should fade,
The only really deadly hurt
    Is this which sin hath made !

To love and serve Thee when I try,
    Oh, bless the weak endeavour !
And listen to my fervent cry—
    " Forsake me not for ever ! "

Even should it prove Thy just decree
    To smite with suffering sore—
Hereafter may I dwell with Thee
    Redeemed for evermore !

SPRING FANCIES.

I WILL lie by the side of this glassy stream
　Where the clear bright waters gently glide,
And give free way to my spirit's dream,
　And the flush of its joy in the sweet spring tide.
Around me is sounding the insect hum,
　Which tells of gladness! and many a bird,
Whose carol in winter time was dumb,
　'Mid the pale-green hazel leaves is heard.

As, reclined on this grassy bank, I gaze
　Up into the smiling azure sky,
How soft is the air which around me plays,
　How limpid the wavelets dancing by!
While the pensive flowers which fringe the shore
　Bend their lovely head (as if whispering)
" We shall droop 'neath the frost and snow no more!
　The cuckoo has brought us back joy and spring!"

See, the ice-bound rivulet is free!
　Free and unshackled by Winter's chain:
Shadowed o'er by the silvery hawthorn tree,
　Whose blossoms are scenting each deep green lane
Where the wild crab blushes so softly mingle
　Their brilliant pink with the pearly May,
And the violets, hidden in glen and dingle,
　Ope their sweet blue eyes to the light of day.

Yon fairy child, with a fawn-like speed,
　O'er the daisy-spangled mead is bounding,
And scarce in his reckless glee gives heed
　To the fragrant things his steps surrounding.

E'en thus, ever thus, in youth's prideful reign
    Are the treasures of life unnoted nigh,
For which weary hearts may sigh in vain
    When their vernal season hath long passed by.

The murmuring stream sings its lullaby,
    And slumber will steal o'er my senses soon,
For the wandering bee, as he glances by,
    Hath wooed me to sleep by his pleasant tune,
And the butterfly's rainbow wing flits near,
    Fanning my upturn'd face and brow,
So beautiful in his wild career,
    As he sips the sweets from each flower and bough.

Let me dream that the fondly loved are near,
    Whose images dwell in my secret soul,
Let the lost and the parted, the true appear,
    Summoned hither by fancy's strong control ;
While their well-known voices thrill again
    On our raptured senses, as of yore :
Oh, could I behold them ! the thought is pain,
    Away ! away ! I must dream no more.

LINES

WRITTEN JULY, 1871.

YES ; we lived there like birds in a bower,
    Where the rose bushes bloomed at our feet,
And though sorrow was mixed with each hour
    Yet affection still rendered them sweet.
The lovely and loved must all perish,
    Too well do we know 'tis earth's doom,
But the hopes which so fondly we cherish,
    Come from heaven to lighten our gloom.

By the calm beauteous lake, while reclining,
  We watched where the white lilies float,
While the bright golden fishes lay shining,
  Of their cups making each one a boat.
The summer birds gaily were flying,
  And the world seemed with joy to o'erbrim :
Though our bosoms were heavy with sighing,
  And our eyes oft with tear drops were dim.
One stern law rules o'er every existence,
  One sentence o'er all doth pervade,
It is written, with cruel persistence,
  "The brightest and dearest must fade."
Oh world, full of sadness and glory,
  Oh mysteries, hidden above !
Too mournful were life's fitful story,
  But for heart-cheering kindness and love.

———◆———

TWO CHRISTMAS SONGS.

CHRISTMAS time is come again,
  With its voice of joy and mirth !
All Christians join the gladdening strain—
  'Tis the happiest day on earth !
No kindly English heart can beat
  Where'er sad exiles roam,
But responds to that salutation sweet,
  The greeting words at home !
      *   *   *   *   *

Merry, merry Christmas !
  Happy, happy Christmas !
On every side we hear—
  Hark ! the joyous sound !

As the wish goes round,
   Re-echoing far and near!

Christmas time returns once more,
   With some memories sad and drear :
We miss the dear ones gone before,
   Who were wont, this day to cheer ;
But such thoughts should not too much oppress
   Poor pilgrims, heaven-ward bound,
Since an earnest of their happiness
   In this blessed day is found.

CHRISTMAS SONG.

OH! the bright Christmas berries!
   They're the cheeriest sight I know ;
Oh ! the bright scarlet berries,
   So gay 'midst the frost and snow!
Pile the fuel higher! yet higher!
   Fill the room with a cheerful glow ;
Let us sing round the blazing fire,
   And forget all the frost and snow!

Let the music of innocent laughter
   Resound in our festive hall,
And re-echo round beam and rafter,
   Where the dancers' footsteps fall!
Here's a welcome to friend and stranger ;
   Give the humble a share in our store!
Remember the Babe in the manger,
   Who was born 'mongst the lowly and poor !

Replenish each cup and bicker
   With the spirit-reviving wine ;

While the snow falls thicker and thicker,
  Let the light of contentment shine :
And oh! whilst we bless the Giver,
  Who has kept all want from our door,
Think of many who starve and shiver,
  And remember, remember the poor !

———•———

FAREWELL TO THE OLD YEAR !

  FAREWELL old year ! farewell !
    How like a troubled dream
    Already dost thou seem,
  Farewell old year ! farewell !
*   *   *   *   *
  With all thy wealth of blessings,
    With all thy weight of pain !
  With all love's fond caressings,
    Now ended is thy reign !
  With all thy bland professings,
    With many a promise vain,
  With all thy store of blessings,
    Now ended is thy reign !
  Farewell old year ! farewell !

Be thankful unto Heaven
  For all its mercies past !
For sins and wrongs forgiven,
  And may its bounties last !
Perchance some tie is riven—
  Some troubles overcast—
But, trust in gracious Heaven !
  And may its bounties last.
Farewell old year ! farewell !

With firm and thankful spirit,
  The opening year we'll greet ;
And through its varied transit,
  God guide our pilgrim feet !
Alive to others' merit,
  (For kindly thoughts are sweet !)
Thus through the new years' transit,
  God guide our pilgrim feet..
Farewell old year ! farewell !

The new year may be joyous—
  It may be dark and drear—
Whate'er the cup filled for us,
  God bless the coming year !
Trials must hover o'er us—
  Yet falter not !—nor fear !
Whate'er the cup filled for us,
  God bless the opening year !
Farewell old year ! farewell !

ON THE DEATH OF LITTLE TINY,

MY FAVOURITE KING CHARLES SPANIEL.

WE laid her in her lowly bed,
  Bestrewn with ferns and heath ;
And kissed her lovely little head
  So beautiful in death !
Now gone for ever from our sight—
  No loving hand could save !
Dear little loving favourite,
  Sad tears bedew thy grave !
  *   *   *   *   *

Long shall I miss those noiseless feet
   Which constant followed me ;
Or, flying on, with pace so fleet,
   'Twas wonderful to see !
Long shall I miss those soft dark eyes,
   Whose earnest, mute appeal
Spoke of such boundless sympathies
   With·all my heart could feel !

Thanks to that gift so exquisite,
   The limner's blessed art,
I have not lost thee, Tiny, quite—
   Before me still thou art.*
Those silken curls which were my pride,
   I seem to stroke them yet ;
Would thou wert lying by my side,
   My gentle little pet !

Dumb friend ! through many a vanished year
   Of mingled good and ill,
Thy graceful form was ever near,
   My joy and comfort still !
Ah ! those, and those alone who've known
   Fidelity as well,
Can guess my sorrow now thou'rt gone—
   The pain of this farewell !

Auchengrey, 1862.

————◆————

THE WEARY HEART.

AH ! bitter when the weary heart
   Can find no place of rest ;

* Tiny's picture was painted by George Sant, Esq., in her
favourite basket house, as if asleep.

When softest tones and looks impart
No dream of being blest!
When all our world of pleasure lies
In one sad word—the past,
And the remaining gifts we prize
Fade from our grasp too fast.
Ah bitter! when the withered smile
Is feigned, and feign'd in vain;
For can we cheat the heart the while—
Teach it to beat again
With the sweet thrilling consciousness
Of joy which once it knew
When life was fraught with loveliness,
And every scene was new?
Ah, no! the mind whence peace has fled
Where sorrow ceaseless dwells,
Thinks but of hours vanished,
And all life's broken spells!
The softest notes of music give
No pleasure to the ear,
For in the cells of memory live
Strains of the past too dear!
Oh! can they waken as of yore
The pulse which long has slept?
Alas! that bounding glee is o'er
Which once in gladness leapt!
Go! call the gay and lovely round,
Summon the minstrel train!
Let each smooth brow with flowers be crowned
While mirth and pleasure reign—
Bid India's richest jewels glow,
The choicest perfumes find—

And let the red grape's nectar flow
   In golden goblets shrined !
Collect each treasure earth can boast,
   And countless riches pile ;
Gather the things we valued most
   To win one happy smile !
And, granting that all this could be,
   The effort would be vain
When busy thought and memory
   Alike but lead to pain !
So different from life's sweet first hour
   When flattery seemed truth,
And each delusive dream had power
   To charm the mind in youth.
No ! sorrow shuts the avenues
   Which led but to delight—
And faded hope's enchanting hues
   Have lost their rosy light.
Go ! to enforce a joyous mood—
   It is too hard a part ;
The deepest, darkest solitude
   Suits best the weary heart !

———◆———

MARINO FALIERO.

LINES WRITTEN TO ILLUSTRATE A PICTURE REPRESENTING
HIM TAKING A LAST FAREWELL OF ANGIOLINA, HIS
DUCHESS, BEFORE HIS EXECUTION.

"FAREWELL, my beautiful ! condemn me not
   If the foul wrong the slanderer heap'd on thee,
Forgiven by thy calm purity—forgot—
   If the vile Steno's insult madden'd me.

How, unaveng'd, could Zara's conqueror die?
He who, for Venice, shed his blood·to save!
Hear the hoarse murmur! the patricians cry
" The warrior prince must fill a traitor's grave."

" But thou, sweet Angiolina! gentle wife!
    Though bitter thus to leave thee, and alone
In the cold world, the blossom of thy life
    Is in its summer yet ; and, when I'm gone—
When the stern memories of my fated lot
    Shall fade away in the dim mist of years,
Perchance thy weary steps may reach some spot
    Untainted by the haunting trace of tears!

" Dost thou remember when the ' Bucentaur '
    Through the blue Adriatic clave its way,
While shouts, and song, and greetings from the shore
    Hail'd, with acclaim, Marino's festal day,—
Sudden, a thick and murky darkness shrouded
    Our gallant bark, and the haze-mantled land,
The brilliant sky was in a moment clouded,
    And misty vapours hid th' expectant strand?

" My fate was shadow'd forth in omens dark,
    E'en in mine hour of glory there was gloom!
It was between the columns of Saint Mark
    (The spot where evil-doers meet their doom)
That Venice saw Faliero's footstep leave,
    On her loved soil, its first and fatal trace,
When pouring forth in gladness, to receive
    The victor Doge, the chosen of her race ;

" And he, the hero of full many a field,
  Whose skill and courage battled with despair,
Who taught the Saracen and Hun to yield,
  They wait for him upon the Giant's stair;
Not, as in olden time, with pomp to set
  The ducal crown upon his hoary head.
Here let it rest—this mocking coronet—
  A few brief moments more its lustre shed!—

"Ere they shall lift it from the traitor's brow,
  The prince conspirator, who dared to seek
His just revenge for calumnies so low—
  My heart would burst, did it essay to speak—
Thou'st loved me, Angiolina, though thy youth
  Was (haply) ill-assorted with thy lord's;
Yet, in thy peerless virtues, in thy truth,
  I found a jewel, priceless beyond words.

"The air blows freshly through the orange-trees,
  Our clime's bright noon-tide sheds its purest ray,
And o'er the azure waves the healthful breeze
  Curls the Lagune's deep waters, as in play!
But hark! they swarm around my palace gates!
  Yon gazing multitude—one breathing flood!
The victim is prepared—the scaffold waits—
  Nature is calm, while man's athirst for blood!

" The headsman's axe is sharp; but sharper still
  This parting pang, sweet love. I dread not death;
But shuddering fears my anxious bosom fill
  For thee.—No rose is on thy cheek, no breath!

Alas! must I be thankful that I grasp
 In my fond arms but pale unconscious clay,
For the last time her small white hand I clasp,
 The hour is come, I must be firm ; away!

"Support, but wake her not ; this death-like swoon
 Is surely sent in Heaven's mercy now.
O God! that I should hail it as a boon
 To gaze my last upon that pallid brow,
And bless the marble whiteness stealing o'er
 Those lovely features, reft of life and bloom,
The lips, whose accents I shall hear no more
 Until we meet, my own, beyond the tomb."
            *   *   *   *
One wild and passionate embrace. 'Tis o'er,
 The fatal summons comes ; the hollow sound
Of armèd feet approaching to the door.
 His guards in silent pomp the Doge surround.
Erect, majestic, he goes forth in state,
 A sovereign to the last, in regal pride
His madness and his crime to expiate—
 And thus the noble and the aged died!

LAMENT.

THERE is woe on the waters,
 A wail o'er the sea :
And in Venice, fair daughters
 Are weeping for thee!
For the mighty has perished,
 And tarnished his fame,
In the country he cherished
 Disgrace blots his name.

In the hall of the crowned,
　Where his image should be,
His place is disowned,
　A black veil we see,*
Which with sable fold covers
　That dishonourèd space,
And a dark shadow hovers
　O'er the last of his race !
In one wild frenzied hour—
　One hour of deep guilt—
When fierce passion had power
　The proud blood was spilt.
Wise statesman ! true hero !
　And bravest of all !
Ah ! Marino Faliero ;
　Woe, woe, for thy fall !

———

LINES

WRITTEN IN THE FIRST PAGE OF THE " BOOK OF
BEAUTY," IN 1841.

THOU mute remembrancer ! yet speaking one !
　How forcibly thy graceful leaves recall
The speed with which the vanished year hath gone,
　Leaving its trace of change on me and all.
Alas ! kind hearts have ceased to beat, whose worth
　Was deeply cherished in the grateful soul.
The brave the true have passed away from earth,
　And weeping memory mourns their distant goal ;

* The portraits of all the Doges of Venice are to be seen,
save that of " Marino Faliero." A black veil alone marks his
vacant place.

Sorrow keeps watch for them o'er saddened breasts
  The scenes which late they cheered look new and
    strange ;
Powerless, and low, and still, the strong man rests,
  His place is vacant here ; all, all is changed.

      *   *   *   *   *

 Beauty and youth ! how gradually they fade
  'Neath the cold touch of time still withering ;
Oh ! ere their brilliant hues are all decayed
  Seek out those gifts which lasting radiance fling
Athwart the shaded path we all must tread
  When the vain triumphs of our bloom are o'er,
And the gay troop of worshippers have fled
  From those whose fading charms can chain no more
A tear may fall, perchance to think how fond
  The homage was thus won in early years,
But there's a tribute to be sought beyond
  Such transient incense ; then, away with tears.
Ah, why should we lament those witching dreams,
  The wild and passionate emotion woke,
When we remember in our sweetest gleams
  Of bliss, some envious hand the charm had broke.
Ah, why should we so sadly, fondly muse
  O'er all that wealth of love cast at our feet,
Which in past years we scarcely sighed to lose :
  Why do we muse ? because, though sad, 'tis sweet !

      *   *   *   ·*   *

Sweet, though the treasure we so sighed to clasp,
  Almost our own, was rudely torn away ;
Sweet, though escaping from our ardent grasp,
  Our dearest hopes were disappointment's prey.

Yes, in the deep recesses of the heart
  A thousand hidden memories must dwell ;
Our Books of Beauty richly there are shrined,
  And the mysterious past their pages tell.

THEY CANNOT RETURN.

COME to that vale where the wild flowers bloom
    sweetest !
They'll speak to thy heart of the bright years gone
    by ;—
They'll bring thee fond memories back, though thou
    greetest
The coming of spring, alas ! now with a sigh !
Ah, no ! Let me weep for the loved ones departed,
Though vainly and sadly my spirit must yearn
For the tones and the looks which enchantment im-
    parted
To each fair scene of nature.—*They cannot return !*

The nightingale warbles of hope and of gladness ;
The soft breezes whisper of pleasure and peace ;
But my heart knows no answering echo, for sadness
Keeps watch o'er its depths !   Ah ! will sorrow ne'er
    cease ?
No ! no ! though the clear crystal streamlets are
    dancing
Through violet banks, from their beauty I turn !
I miss the soft eyes—the dear voices enhancing
Each vanish'd enjoyment.—*They cannot return !*

HYMN—ADORATION.

O HEAVENLY LORD! how beautiful
  Are all things Thou hast made!
Thy mercies are so plentiful—
  Thy good gifts never fade.
The moon and stars, whose brilliant orbs
  Illume the silent night—
My raptured soul the view absorbs
  In ever new delight.
Hereafter—when the spirit's chain
  From earthly ties is riven—
When, freed from sin's debasing stain,
  The ransomed meet in heaven.
What joy! to sing the Saviour's praise,
  Midst those bright stars to soar—
While angel voices sweetly raise
  Loud pæans evermore!

—◆—

FAITH.

THINE, LORD! all Thine
  This trembling heart would be;
Thy love divine
  From sin has set me free.
Weary, I bent
  Beneath my guilty load;
Now I'm content—
  I lean upon my God!

Blest be Thy name,
  For all Thy mercies given ;
Priceless my claim,
  Through Christ's dear blood to heaven !
In grateful rapture
  My feeble soul essays,
With every creature,
  To sing my song of praise !

Pleasure's vain toys
  Allure, but to beguile ;
Vain are earth's joys
  Without our Maker's smile !
Those who repent,
  And kiss the chastening rod ;
Shall learn content,
  While leaning on our God !

SYMPATHY.

THE heart will oft be lonely !
  No sympathy around ;
There is but One, One only
  In whom love doth abound.
Ah ! why cast we our pearls abroad ?
  Our pearls of heart and soul ?
Why still the guilty conscience load
  With burdens past control ?
It is a weary feeling
  To find no answer given—
To dry the salt tears stealing,
  When vainly we have striven

To wake one thought responding
To those which in us burn—
Well may we be desponding,
Unless to Christ we turn!

———•———

HEAVEN.

WHEN friends long parted meet again,
And happy tears fall down like rain
As to our hearts their forms we strain—
  We cry, "Oh! this is Heaven!"
Or, gazing on some beauteous scene
Where lovely nature smiles serene,
No mournful thoughts to intervene—
  We murmur, "This is Heaven!"

Though earth is full of sin and woe,
God yet hath pleasures to bestow
On fainting pilgrims here below,
  Who struggle on towards Heaven—
But, oh, my soul, what joy for thee
When, from thy load of guilt set free,
To thy dear Saviour thou shalt flee
  And sing, "Oh! this is Heaven!"

———•———

SUPPLICATION.

FORGIVE! O Lord! forgive!
  And hear my hymn of praise—
That Thou hast let me live
  To mend mine erring ways.

Oh ! for a heart to feel
   The mercies Thou dost give,
In worship as I kneel :
   Forgive ! O Lord ! forgive !
*   *   *   *   *
Sustain me, Lord ! sustain !
   And in my dying hour,
When human help is vain,
   Be there in love and power.
When Thou shalt call me home,
   Though sharp the parting pain,
My Saviour Jesus, come !
   And in that hour sustain.

WORDS

WRITTEN FOR JACQUES BLUMENTHAL'S BEAUTIFUL
MELODY, "LES DEUX ANGES."

"NEVER more ! ah ! never more !"
   Sighs my soul in bitter pain—
" Never more ! ah ! never more !
   Can I taste such bliss again !"
Then my paths seemed strewn with flowers,
   Youth and love enwreathing—
Pleasure winged the fleeting hours,
   Rapture round me breathing.

" Evermore ! yes ! evermore :"
   Hark ! a seraph's voice is telling—
" Evermore ! yes ! evermore !
   Joy in Heaven is dwelling."
Dim foretastes of our happy state
   Are granted unto mortals,

They cannot enter glory's gate
    Till sorrow opes the portals.

Nevermore! no! nevermore!
    Sinning or repenting—
Earth's sad conflict will be o'er,
    And each vain lamenting.
Life's vicissitudes will cease
    Beyond death's lonely river;
There—loving hearts shall rest in peace,
    Adoring God for ever!

VOICES.

'Twas on a Sabbath evening,
    Helpless and ill I lay—
Musing on death and Heaven,
    Ready to pass away.
The silent room seemed filling
    With forms I loved of yore—
My fainting bosom thrilling
    With whispers o'er and o'er.
" Soon thou mayest reach thy spirit's home—
Quickly come! oh! come! come!"

So sweetly—sadly calling—
    Methought I must obey!
A solemn awe was falling
    Upon the parting day.
But earthly love was stronger
    Then each beseeching tone—
I prayed to tarry longer
    With him who is my own.

"No! not yet! I cannot come
Without him to my spirit's home!"

July, 1867.

FORBEARANCE.

WHO knows not how the spirit grieves,
    That finds deceit in one beloved?
Trust not the friend who once deceives—
    Whose falsehood is too clearly proved.
'Tis well we should condemn—yet pause
    Ere hotly we the wrong resent,
For ah! what misery they cause
    Who think no erring ones repent!

Alas! it is a cruel blow
    To find our confidence betrayed—
Our loyal trust at once laid low,
    And all our faith a ruin made.
Yet think—how often have *we* broke
    Our vows to God! the Lord of all!
Too oft revoked the words we spoke,
    And failed to answer at His call!

Yes! thus the Friend of friends we treat:
    Not once—but constantly we err;
Yet hourly, with His pity sweet
    He deigns to be our comforter!
The penitent He'll gently spare,
    And crushes not the contrite heart.
Dear Saviour! teach me to forbear:
    Teach me the blest forgiving part!

Rather to bear the cruel jeer—
  The inuendo—cutting deep—
The bitter treachery to hear,
  Than one resentful feeling keep !
Though all in vain we may have striven
  Our meed of grateful love to earn—
He who has countless sins forgiven,
  Bids us forgiving lessons learn !

CHEER UP—SAD HEART.

CHEER up, sad heart !
  Nothing lasts long—
Hope for to-morrow, if grief claim to-day
  List to the comfort
    Contained in my song—
Sorrow and sighing shall all pass away !

  Yes ! but oh ! when ?
  Life is so dreary !
Parting so bitter !—and suffering so keen !
  Rest to the mourner,
    And sleep to the weary—
Such all the comfort your pity would mean.

  Comfort ! ah, yes :
  But joy in the distance—
Joy never dreamt of, to thee shall be given ;
  Love in its purity—
    Blissful existence :
Be thou but patient, and live on for Heaven !

  Cast away from thee
    Earth's grovelling wishes—
Aspire to the height which true piety wins ;

All here must fail thee,
    Ambition and riches!
When this world fades — then the real one
    begins.   .

———

MERCY.

PITY all the sad of heart!
    Think thine own dark hour may come—
Ne'er forget the Christian's part :
    Else no peace shall bless thy home.
Mercy is a holy thing !
    Think without it what were we ?—
Lost ! but for Christ's ransoming :
    Then—like Him—let's strive to be,
Full of gentlest sympathy
    With our fellow-creatures' woe,
Whatsoe'er the cause may be—
    'Tis the least we can bestow !

Well may wounded spirits shrink
    From the eyes that coldly scan—
Love should rivet every link,
    Kindness plead for man with man !
If the suffering come from sin,
    Censure not with mien so stern ;
How shall we forgiveness win,
    If we from our brother turn ?
Then—with accents soft and mild,
    Generous hand and helpful brain,
Welcome ever sorrow's child,
    So shall we God's blessing gain !

A HYMN.

GOD Almighty! Heavenly Father!
   Thou to whom all creatures bow—
When the storms of life shall gather,
   Let Thy hand avert the blow:
Thou, the God of all the living!
   Who dost know our grief and sin—
With temptations daily striving,
   Let our prayers a refuge win!

When the world its most alluring
   Aspect wears to heedless youth,
Teach our hearts Thy joy enduring!
   That of holy faith and truth!
Fainting 'neath the heavy pressure
   Of our trials dark and sad,
Thou, whose power is without measure,
   Thou alone can'st make us glad!

Elevate men's restless spirit,
   Ever sighing and in vain;
Show us how we may inherit
   All the peace we've failed to gain.
Heavenly Father! ever dwelling
   In Thy glory! bend Thine ear!
Hear Thy suppliant children telling
   All their woe—in pity hear!

———

WRITTEN IN A SUFFERING HOUR.

MY Saviour! in the hour of pain—
When every nerve is on the strain,

When anguish racks the weary frame,
And suffering the spirits tame—
How weak, how wretched should we be,
Unless our thoughts could rest on Thee!

What does the cold, vain world avail
When health and strength alike must fail?
And e'en affection's warmest glow,
No lasting comfort can bestow;
But Christ will be our stay in all
Which human frailty can befall.

O Thou, who didst so suffer here,
My sufferings to me endear—
If through their means my soul may be
More closely brought to cling to Thee.
Be Thou my guardian and my rest,
And that of him I love the best!

SIMPLE WORDS OF COMFORT
(ADDRESSED TO ONE IN DEEP SUFFERING).

I CLING to Thee, Lord Jesus!
    I humbly cling to Thee!
To Him who knows and sees us
    Wherever we may be.

In all my deep affliction,
    In all my hours of woe;
It is no dream nor fiction,
    That to Him I may go

For comfort and instruction,
    For pardon and for peace,
To save me from destruction,
    And bid my sorrows cease.

So numberless my errors,
   Well may they bow me down ;
But love shall calm my terrors—
   His love in mercy shown !

On my Redeemer leaning
   When fails my parting breath—
His arm will then be screening
   My soul from pangs of death.

I've known life's sweetest pleasures,
   Though grief has made them dim ;
No name my heart so treasures
   As the blest name of Him,

Our Saviour! the Lord Jesus !
   Who doth from sin set free ;
Who knows us, and who sees us ;
   And loves both you and me!

———◆———

ALONE.

ALL must yield up their breath,
   And cross the gulf alone—
The dreary gulf of death
   Which leads to shores unknown.
Yes! all—the true, the fond,
   The idols of each heart—
To reach the world beyond,
   Must journey hence apart!

It is a mournful truth :
   The dearest and the best,
The loved—in age or youth—
   All lonely is their rest !

The closely-linked in mind—
 The soul's most cherished one;
The fair, the bright, the kind,
 Must perish—and alone!

It is a thought of woe—
 A pang too deep for speech :
Yet all this grief must know—
 Ah! let it wisdom teach!
And while the loved are here,
 Be it our fond employ
To brighten their career,
 And deck their paths with joy.

If, in our Saviour's love
 We place our stedfast trust,
Far less our fear 'twill move
 The fiat " Dust to dust!"
As through the shadowy vale
 Our trembling steps we wend,
Our courage need not fail
 With Jesus for our friend!

Oh! then—while health and youth
 Still crown the flowery way,
Seek we the path of truth—
 And God's command obey!
So—yielding up our breath
 To Him the boon who gave,
No sting shall be in death—
 No terror in the grave!

———◆———

SABBATH BELLS.

SWEET sabbath bells! so loud and clear!
 Pealing o'er valley and o'er hill!
What heavenly music to mine ear!
 They seem to say, " Why linger still?
Come to God's temple while ye may,
And prayer will steal your griefs away!

" Haste to God's temple! there to raise
 The song warm springing from the heart—
The incense of your grateful praise,
 In, which all Christians bear a part.
Hear our glad summons, and obey!
The angels join ye as ye pray!

" Come to that holy, solemn place,
 Where peace and soul-felt comfort dwell ;
The home of each celestial grace,
 Where mercy's beams all clouds dispel!
Haste to God's temple while ye may!
The angels join the meek who pray!"

LINES.

LORD JESUS! who art ever near
 The soul that suffering flies to Thee,
Do Thou in mercy bend Thine ear,
 And this frail form from anguish free!

I

But if it be the Almighty will
  That I this torture should endure—
Let thoughts of Thee, impatience still,
  And make Thy word of promise sure!

Dear martyred Lord! what is my pain
  To that which Thou didst bear for me?
Thou who didst gloriously sustain
  The whole world's sin on Calvary:
Yet—fainting, trembling, do I cry
  Whene'er my feeble strength is spent.
Oh! listen to me as I sigh,
  And make me with Thy love content.

SELF-QUESTIONINGS.

How shall I feel when life is surely fading?
  And few brief hours on earth for me remain?
When death's dark wings all brightness shall be
    shading,
  And tears from kindly eyes are shed in vain.
Shall I feel hopeless, lost, and terrified?
No! not while Jesus tarries by my side!

Leave me not, Jesus, I have truly loved Thee!
  Though other things alas! I've loved too well!
For this Thou hast chastised—Thou hast reproved me,
  And to all former joys I've bade farewell;
All save affection! mingling with my breath
That love defying change, and strong as death.

How shall I feel? O God, I do beseech Thee,
    In that dark fearsome valley, be my guide!
And let the sweet words in Thy gospel teach me,
    With Thy sure promise to rest satisfied.
Believe in Jesus Christ, poor trembling heart,
Then all thy fears and sorrows shall depart.

DESOLATION.

"Withdraw not Thou Thy mercy from me, O Lord! Let
Thy loving-kindness and Thy truth alway preserve me!"

PSALM xl. 14.

LEAVE me not, Jesus,
    I totter—I fall:
My case is so grievous,
    But Thou know'st it all.
My frailty, my sorrow,
    My weakness and pain,
Oh, where shall I borrow
    The strength to sustain?

Leave me not, Jesus,
    When we go astray,
When all we love leave us,
    Do Thou point the way
To sweet consolation,
    By Thee alone given,
In my desolation:
    Oh, guide me to Heaven.

My life is so dreary,
    In loneliness left;
My poor heart so weary,
    Of all joy bereft.

O Saviour! O Jesus!
　　Respond to its call:
My burthen is grievous,
　　But Thou know'st it all.

While thus sadly weeping
　　An angel sings near,
" Thy Saviour is keeping
　　Account of each tear.
O'er life's stormy ocean
　　The tempest shall cease;
Grief leads to devotion,
　　To pardon, and peace."

　　　　　　　　　　December, 1872.

MAY THOUGHTS AT CHETNOLE.

METHOUGHT this weary heart was dead,
　　Dead, in its living grave;
That from the treasures vanished
　　No relic hope could save.
But God is better than our thought,
　　And in this sweet spring tide,
I find the world with beauty fraught,
　　Still dear ones by my side.

How exquisite the opening leaves,
　　The wealth of lovely flowers:
Fresh strength the o'erwrought brain receives,
　　Living such life as ours.
The sweet birds warble midst the flush
　　Of orchard's rosy bloom,
The blackbird, nightingale, and thrush,
　　Fill earth's vast concert room

With melodies which breathe of praise
  To the Great God on high :
Oh, in these gladsome vernal days,
  How soft grows every sigh.
The weary, desolate, and worn,
  Whose eyes sad tears made dim,
If meekly they their cross have borne,
  Sure refuge find with Him
Who pities our infirmities,
  And sees us as we are :
In all life's dark perplexities
  There's but one guiding star.
Ay, in this transitory home,
  Our springs will soon be told,
But in the glorious world to come
  None will grow sad or old.
No change, no partings there will be
  To rend the soul in twain,
But oh, the thought is ecstacy !
  The loved will meet again.

WERTHEIMER, LEA AND CO., PRINTERS, CIRCUS PLACE, FINSBURY CIRCUS.

www.ingramcontent.com/pod-product-compliance
Lightning Source LLC
Chambersburg PA
CBHW030622270326
41927CB00007B/1280